Rapid Transformation Therapy

A Guided Process for Healing Trauma and Awakening the Light Within

by Marianne Rolland Ph.D., LMSW

BALBOA
PRESS
A DIVISION OF HAY HOUSE

Copyright © 2016 Marianne Rolland Ph.D., LMSW.

All rights reserved. No part of this book may be used or reproduced by any means, graphic, electronic, or mechanical, including photocopying, recording, taping or by any information storage retrieval system without the written permission of the author except in the case of brief quotations embodied in critical articles and reviews.

Balboa Press books may be ordered through booksellers or by contacting:

Balboa Press
A Division of Hay House
1663 Liberty Drive
Bloomington, IN 47403
www.balboapress.com
1 (877) 407-4847

Because of the dynamic nature of the Internet, any web addresses or links contained in this book may have changed since publication and may no longer be valid. The views expressed in this work are solely those of the author and do not necessarily reflect the views of the publisher, and the publisher hereby disclaims any responsibility for them.

The author of this book does not dispense medical advice or prescribe the use of any technique as a form of treatment for physical, emotional, or medical problems without the advice of a physician, either directly or indirectly. The intent of the author is only to offer information of a general nature to help you in your quest for emotional and spiritual well-being. In the event you use any of the information in this book for yourself, which is your constitutional right, the author and the publisher assume no responsibility for your actions.

Any people depicted in stock imagery provided by Getty Images are models, and such images are being used for illustrative purposes only. Certain stock imagery © Getty Images.

Print information available on the last page.

ISBN: 978-1-5043-6745-5 (sc)
ISBN: 978-1-5043-6746-2 (e)

Balboa Press rev. date: 09/12/2018

Dedication

To all beings who are courageous enough
to come full-face with self.

"Who looks outside, dreams. Who looks inside, awakens."

—Carl Jung

DISCLAIMER

This book is designed to provide information and motivation to our readers. It is sold with the understanding that the author(s) and publisher are not engaged to render any type of medical, psychological, legal, or any other kind of professional advice. This book is not meant to be used, nor should it be used, to diagnose or treat any medical condition. For diagnosis or treatment of any medical problem, consult your own physician. The publisher and author(s) are not responsible for any specific health needs that may require medical supervision and are not liable for any damages or negative consequences to any person reading or following the information in this book from any treatment, action, application or preparation.

Neither the publisher nor the individual author(s) shall be liable for any physical, psychological, emotional, financial or commercial damages, including but not limited to special, incidental, consequential or other damages. References are provided for informational purposes only and do not constitute endorsement of any websites or other sources. Some names and identifying details have been changed to protect the privacy of individuals.

TABLE OF CONTENTS

Prologue: A White Raven Invitation x

Chapter 1: The Genesis of Rapid Transformation Therapy ..13

Chapter 2: Defining RTT as a Method of Recovery 20

Chapter 3: Understanding Emotional Energy—A Journey to the Core of Your Being 38

Chapter 4: Participatory Soul Retrieval 55

Chapter 5: RTT for PTSD, Emotional Trauma, and Abuse ...77

Chapter 6: RTT for Addictions and Their Aftermath.......... 114

Chapter 7: Caretakers Discover the Benefits of RTT 139

Chapter 8: Physical Symptoms Shift and Heal 153

Chapter 9: Understanding and Clearing Energy Attachments 170

Chapter 10: Maintaining a Transformed State of Inner Peace 178

Chapter 11: Tips for Practitioners and Individuals Who Want to Try RTT..192

Chapter 12: Healing Our Selves to Contribute to Healing the World 207

Appendix A: RTT's Connection to Other Treatment Modalities/Theories 217

Appendix B: Floyd's White Raven Story 224

Appendix C: A Reflection From an RTT Participant 233

Appendix D: White Raven Center Tool Kit 239

Appendix E: Recommended Reading List 252

Appendix F: Acknowledgements 253

A White Raven Invitation

Imagine you walk into a cedar ceremonial house. A fire burns brightly in the center, and a Native medicine man waits to tell you a story. When he looks at you, you feel like he is looking through you and sees your pain. He begins by drumming softly and singing a song that reaches deep inside your heart. Feelings erupt within you, yet you feel safe. You feel a sense of belonging and that you matter. You feel like a child being nurtured by a loving human being whom you trust.

He draws you deeper into his song. In the darkness and the fire, for a split second, you are certain you see Raven looking at you. Then Raven transforms back into the medicine man. As he sings, you allow yourself to relax and surrender to the moment.

In the beginning, Raven was white. He found human beings living on the earth in darkness, hiding away and afraid because they could not see what was around them. Raven felt sorry for these human beings, so he set out to bring them. In the process he flew through a smokehole in the sky chief's house, singeing his white feathers to black.

Raven was baffled by mankind's fear of darkness. He wondered why humans were so disconnected from their true selves. Raven's message is to help us wake up to the truth that we alone have the power to transform our lives. He tells us that to awaken the within, we must transcend the darkness. As we shift inside and restore our inner balance, we diminish the power we have given to the darkness.

Guided by the spirit of Raven's light, our White Raven Center in Anchorage, Alaska came into being. Our mission is to create opportunities for healing on deep levels, opening our heart centers and awakening the within. We learn to recognize that what Raven tells us is true: We are not our pain. We are not our traumatic life experiences. We are not our stories. We have the ability to transform our lives and dissolve the power we have allowed the darkness to have over us. We learn to set ourselves free as Raven has always been. Our shines wherever we are. Raven walks the darkness without fear, and so can we. As we let go of our fear, we walk away from the ceremonial house fully conscious of who we are.

If you're interested in reading an expanded version of the White Raven story as told by my husband, Floyd, turn to Appendix B.

"Listening to and understanding our inner sufferings will resolve most of the problems we encounter."

—Thich Nhat Hanh

Chapter 1

The Genesis of Rapid Transformation Therapy

In 1977 I was twenty-four years old, a social worker living and working in rural Alaska Native villages. I lived alone in an isolated cabin with no running water. Outside temperatures sometimes dropped to 60 degrees below zero. My assignment was to provide comprehensive social services to eight villages and two larger communities, all linked by a regional hub road system.

My training provided me with the skills to be a good listener, to have compassion for others' experiences and points of view without judgment, to reach out to others who were suffering, and to seek potential resources. To do all of that, I had to be willing to knock on the doors of total strangers in a culture foreign to my own life experience.

Soon, I realized I was a welcomed guest. My first friend was Elizabeth, an elder within the community. As we sat at her kitchen table sipping hot tea and nibbling on pilot bread crackers, she poured her heart out to me in her broken English. She told me horrific stories of human cruelty as she shared the hurts and suffering of her children, grandchildren, and great-grandchildren. "Drinking caused all of the bad things that people do to each other," she told me.

Despite her emotional pain I also sensed her hope, her inner calm, and the belief that things would get better. As trust was nurtured between us and our hearts bonded, we became a team working together for the betterment and healing of the community.

I soon met more elders and became overwhelmed with the depth of their grief and suffering. I recognized their desperation and yet sensed the wisdom among these people. The elders repeatedly expressed gratitude for the opportunity to be heard and stressed that life in the villages had become imbalanced. They wanted the pain to end, and so did I.

I wasn't aware then that the majority of the people in the villages were suffering from repressed trauma and post-traumatic stress disorder (PTSD). I also wasn't aware that their stories were activating repressed feelings within my own psyche and body.

Nothing in my formal education had adequately prepared me to work with emotional trauma, so I returned to the University of Washington to earn master's and doctorate degrees in social work. When it came time to complete my dissertation project, I was drawn again to the elders to gain a deeper understanding of their historical perspective on human traumas and traditional ways of healing. The elders, who are considered the wisdom-keepers for their tribes, repeatedly gave me the message that healing is only possible if you include the dimension of. A middle-aged man trained in the traditional methods explained it this way:

"In the old days, everything was in balance. Everything was considered through a ual lens or realm. The medicine man, shaman, or sleep doctor was at the center of keeping things in balance. It was a whole and balanced system and it was highly ual. Each person learned how they were to be, to interact within that well-defined system."

In traditional Native American communities, daily rituals and ceremonies were practiced to help maintain that balance. Everybody watched out for everyone else's well-being. The elders also told me that "true healing comes from within." I was intrigued by the concept of healing from within, and yet, I couldn't find anyone to show me how to do it. I sensed that the elders knew, yet bringing long-forgotten traditional practices into the modern world was difficult. They all spoke in broken English, and they thought primarily in their Native language.

Despite the language barrier, I witnessed my elder friends releasing intense emotional pain. Even though they were isolated and blocked from using their traditional practices to ease suffering in the larger community, they allowed for the flow of great emotional energy in themselves, with me as their witness. They taught me the value of being present, and the power of having human witness to our pain and deepest suffering. I was honored and moved to the core of my being.

This experience planted a seed within me about what we all might need in order to heal our emotional pain. The concept of "balance" within the individual, the family, and the community became a guide for me as I gathered elements of what eventually became a very specific healing process.

Healing PTSD Is Possible

"I do not view post-traumatic stress disorder as pathology to be managed, suppressed, or adjusted to, but the result of a natural process gone awry. Healing trauma requires a direct experience of the living, feeling, knowing organism."

—Peter A. Levine

Twenty years later, in 1997, my husband, Floyd—himself an Alaska Native—returned home after attending a workshop in Seattle with a national expert on healing the family. A Vietnam veteran and survivor of childhood neglect and sexual abuse, Floyd asked this expert, "Is there a cure for PTSD?"

Without hesitation, the expert said, "No, there is no cure. You just have to learn to live with it."

Floyd looked at the man in shock. My husband had carried so much hope that one day, he would achieve peace within himself. Those words—"there is no cure"—devastated him.

When he came home and shared the story with me, I felt my body tighten and begin to shake. "He is dead wrong!" I blurted out angrily, "There *is* a cure for PTSD! I know there is!" Partially as a result of what I had experienced in the villages during my years of social work, my inner knowingness screamed that it couldn't possibly be true that there was no cure. So I trusted that the cure did exist, and I set a clear intent to discover "the way."

Two months later, I met a woman who was practicing a way of healing from the inside out. This teacher showed me that to heal trauma and restore balance to our beings, we must connect with the place inside of us where we most deeply suppress our pain.

We access those repressed core emotions through our breath. With focused practice, I came to understand that there was a way anyone could access deep emotions as I had watched the elders do so many years before. I became passionate about my discovery. I wanted to help the whole world heal.

I started with my immediate family, including myself. We had all experienced our share of trauma, and I finally began to see why the pain of the people I counseled as a social worker had activated so much of my own repressed inner pain. At last, a way to truly heal from within had been revealed, and I knew I would be working with this method for the rest of my life.

Fast-forward to 2014. Floyd, our dedicated team of facilitators, and I have witnessed hundreds of people transform their lives. We have spent the past eighteen years expanding the process of accessing core emotions through the breath into a comprehensive emotional healing process that we have come to call "Rapid Transformation Therapy" or "RTT." In addition to this breathwork, RTT also draws upon wisdom from my elder teachers, including Grandmother Berniece Falling Leaves, Rita Blumenstein, and Martin High Bear, and methodologies from across a variety of disciplines including social work, regression therapy, energy medicine, traditional Western therapy, and both indigenous and Eastern practices.

With the aim of restoring balance, we have discovered repeatedly that unlocking emotional energy in the human body and allowing it to release will diminish PTSD symptoms and pain—both physical pain and emotional pain. This is as true for war veterans and those who have acute symptoms from trauma and abuse as it is for those experiencing less-acute symptoms due to grief, breakups, fears, and any number of life's difficulties.

Symptoms don't have to be "managed." In our experience they can be eliminated or, at a minimum, dramatically diminished. Healing is possible. There *is* a cure for PTSD, and it doesn't require expensive treatments or becoming dependent upon pharmaceuticals.

RTT is unlike anything else I have witnessed or experienced in my lifelong journey as a helping professional. I founded the White Raven Center in Anchorage, Alaska to create an opportunity for others to heal from repressed emotional trauma and to restore balance within their own beings. I wrote this book to share a part of my healing journey with you and potentially offer hope where none exists.

My heart's grandest desire is to experience peace on Earth. I know this can never happen until each one of us returns to a state of inner balance. My sincere hope is that the healing methodology presented here will be used as a gift to discover your own inner peace and balance, and to assist others if you are in a helping profession.

"Your life
is yours to live,
no matter how you choose
to live it.
When you do not
think about how you
intend to live it,
it lives you.
When you occupy it,
step into it consciously,
you live it."

—Gary Zukav

Chapter 2

Defining RTT as a Method of Recovery

When we refuse to express our feelings, where do they go? Do emotions just disappear on their own? Does time really heal all wounds, as the popular adage would have us believe?

Psychological research—as well as decades of people sitting across from therapists in offices all over the world—has taught us that many of our old traumas and hurts do not just disappear like magic. They stay with us, and the emotions we feel become stored and stagnant in the body. These "frozen" emotions significantly limit our ability to heal and experience life fully and joyfully.

Sometimes life events reactivate those old traumas and hurts, bringing them to the surface and causing us to react in ways that may seem out of proportion to the event. Have you ever become very upset about something and not understood why? Chances are, you were reacting more to emotions buried deep inside you than to your current circumstances.

At the White Raven Center, people access their repressed emotions, release them, and heal their old traumas and hurts. Facilitators guide and encourage each individual—either in a private session or a group workshop—to allow those emotions to break loose from within. The outcome is a transformation of stored, dense energies, ultimately resulting in greater well-being, personal authenticity, and inner peace.

We have found that RTT can often facilitate dramatic and quantum healing in a very short period of time. While not a

Defining RTT as a Method of Recovery

"quick fix"—RTT is a method of deep emotional processing that requires commitment—it has helped many people accelerate the release of immense emotional pain in a way that traditional talk therapy rarely provides. Although deep emotional processes are the cornerstone of Rapid Transformation Therapy, the methodology requires us to also shift our thoughts, beliefs and attitudes. These are all powerful elements in being able to maintain the relief that you experience in your RTT sessions.

In the pages that follow you will read about how RTT works, including the stories of a number of our clients who credit the process for quite literally saving their lives. These people include veterans with clinically diagnosed PTSD, men and women who have experienced violence and sexual abuse, people who were victims of tremendous neglect as children, those who have struggled with all sorts of addictions from drugs and alcohol to pornography, people who have gone through horrendous loss, and individuals who have felt unseen, unloved, angry, afraid, or hurt at some point in their lives.

"Wait a minute," you might be thinking. "Isn't that all of us?" Yes—who hasn't been hurt? Who isn't holding on to some pain fromthepast? For thisreason, you're almost certain to identify with someone's story as you continue reading. The experiences include grief, divorce, rejection, insecurities, bullying and intolerance, suicidal feelings, addictions, self-destructive behaviors, injuries, violence, and abuse (emotional, mental, physical and sexual).

As you'll see from the examples provided, RTT can help you decrease dependencies on prescription drugs and other substances, diminish the full range of symptoms related to PTSD, alleviate core issues causing addiction, open to your spiritual gifts, access your body's natural capacity to heal itself, and awaken the light that resides within.

Through RTT, we have seen people become more connected to all of life and more open to giving and receiving love. They have been able to regain their sense of balance and discover a profound ability to feel unconditional love for self and others. They have experienced the deep bliss of coming home to themselves.

In order to thrive, each of these individuals first had to allow themselves to access repressed emotional pain through the breath and uncover the blocked memories connected to their life's traumatic events.

The Truth About PTSD and Emotions

According to the Diagnostic and Statistical Manual of Mental Disorders (fourth edition, DSM-IV-TR), "The essential feature of post-traumatic stress disorder is the development of characteristic symptoms following exposure to an extreme traumatic stressor involving direct personal experience of an event that involves actual or threatened death or serious injury, or other threat to one's physical integrity; or witnessing an event that involves death, injury, or a threat to the physical integrity of another person; or learning about unexpected or violent death, serious harm, or threat of death or injury experienced by a family member or other close associate."[1]

The diagnosis of PTSD is generally regarded as a condition that manifests among soldiers who have experienced and witnessed the repeated traumas characterized by a state of war. It has also become common knowledge that survivors of any major catastrophic event, such as the destruction of the World Trade Center on 9/11/2001, may be afflicted with PTSD. In the early 1990s, those providing services to American Indian and Alaska Native populations began to recognize that a high proportion of their clientele were suffering from the

---

[1] American Psychiatric Association, Diagnostic and Statistical Manual of Mental Disorders, 4th Edition, DSM-IV-TR, (American Psychiatric Association, 2000), 463.

same symptoms as those who had been exposed to war and catastrophic events.

The truth is that any kind of trauma may result in minor, moderate, or even acute symptoms of PTSD. In my work over the years with generations of people, I have come to the conclusion that nearly everyone suffers to some degree from repressed emotions that may be attributed to PTSD. Nearly everyone—even those of us who are leading what appear to be relatively easy and comfortable lives—has undergone some kind of trauma, and that trauma has almost certainly had lasting emotional and physical effects. I consider those effects to be a form of PTSD. However, repeated trauma such as prolonged sexual, mental or physical abuse may result in what some clinicians now refer to as *complex* PTSD.

Nevertheless, we cannot compare the effects of one trauma with another. The impact of a traumatic event on a human being does not differentiate between "levels" or "types" of experience. As children, we are much more vulnerable to what might, to adults, seem an inconsequential hurt. We hold on to those hurts into adulthood, and they affect our behaviors from a place outside of our awareness.

We don't know, for example, if harsh words spoken to a child are any more or less traumatic to the soul than an experience of sexual molestation. We don't know if emotional abandonment by parents is any less devastating than harsh physical abuse. We cannot judge how much someone else feels about a traumatic event. We cannot create a scale and say, "You're hurting too much over that because it 'shouldn't' have been that traumatic."

We all have varying levels of resilience. One person may not be affected by what wounds another person to the core. And that doesn't necessarily mean one individual is stronger than the other. It simply means we all have variations as to how we experience the events in our lives.

Common Symptoms of PTSD Include:

- Repeated and disturbing memories from the past
- Feeling as if the traumatic experience were happening all over again
- Sleeplessness
- Chronic stomach problems
- Hypervigilance, regardless of the circumstance
- Feeling numb most of the time
- Ongoing depression
- Feeling detached from other people
- Not being able to have loving feelings for those who are closest to you
- Being intensely emotionally reactive
- Frequent angry outbursts
- Repeated and disturbing dreams
- Guilt to the extreme
- Shame that binds
- Feeling as if you are not always in your body
- Uncontrollable crying
- Loneliness even when surrounded by those you love
- Dissociation
- Occupational instability
- Memory disturbances
- Family discord that feels like the norm
- Feeling tense all the time
- Major trust issues
- Chronic headaches
- Difficulty concentrating

In order to survive our traumatic life events, society tells us to "put it out of your mind," "forget about it," "don't dwell on the past," "think positively," "stay in the moment," and all sorts of other seemingly wonderful pieces of advice. As a result we discount our internal experience and pretend our feelings don't exist, while those same feelings eat away at us from the inside out.

Soul Loss and Soul Retrieval

One further effect of trauma/PTSD is that we experience the loss of parts of our soul. Frequently, clients report that the RTT process creates a feeling of "coming home." This is because RTT helps people reconnect with their souls—something that a great many people need without even knowing it.

For centuries, indigenous peoples around the world have understood that there is an intrinsic and powerful connection between the body and the soul. They have also understood that traumas cause us to disconnect from aspects of our souls, and this disconnect can negatively impact our physical, mental, emotional and spiritual health. This is the soul's unconscious attempt at self-preservation. It's like a non-physical "running away" of a part of the self, to avoid feeling pain that is too much to bear in the moment. This is a frequent occurrence for children because we are so vulnerable when we're young. It's no surprise that so many of us feel as though something is missing in our lives . . . *because it actually is.* No wonder we feel lonely and search for something to "fill us up."

This understanding of the relationship between the body and the soul is one of many ways in which our method draws upon traditional Native American and worldwide indigenous practices. These are combined with Eastern traditions and conventional Western healing methodologies, giving us access to the best of all worlds.

It is my experience, for example, based upon decades of healing work with thousands of people, that all disease and illness has some degree of soul loss at its root. Whether or not you believe in actual soul loss, reconnecting with parts of you that have gone into hiding due to trauma is a process that clearly works. What you call it is up to you. At White Raven Center we respect all belief systems, and we don't impose our beliefs on the participants in our workshops—or on you as our reader. We simply ask you to surrender to the process because that is the only way you can reap the benefits.

You will read more about soul loss and soul retrieval in chapter 4, and stories of soul retrieval during RTT will be shared throughout the book. This is a fundamental element of RTT that seems to occur naturally during the process.

RTT and Spirituality

RTT is connected deeply to our spirituality, as it is a process of caring for and loving ourselves in a way we may never have done before. You don't need to adhere to any particular set of spiritual beliefs for RTT to be beneficial to you. All you need is the desire to feel better, live a fuller life, and feel at peace. The process of RTT is facilitated by the level of openness we have to our own spirit and inner spiritual guidance.

The spirit is pure and clear, possessing no darkness or negativity; it has no agenda and no limitations. The spirit has no expectations and as we open fully to it, we awaken to our light within. In doing so, we discover a sense of calm and acceptance.

There may be some information in this book that differs from your personal belief system. You may feel uncomfortable and challenged at times by what you read. The information might bring up fear or even anger in you. If this is the case, please know that repressed energies are being activated. If you're open and willing, all of those emotions can be worked through in the process of RTT itself.

As our friend and fellow author Seth Taylor shares, "Christian traditions are broad in their perception of the spiritual world, but in many popular forms of Christianity today, there is a misperception that material from the deep psyche, as it surfaces and manifests in raw and toxic forms before exiting the body, is actually a manifestation of spiritual demons or perhaps even the devil or Satan. There is a fear that this is a type of possession, and this fear then invalidates their belief that they have indeed been 'saved.'"

Regardless of this belief, Christians who work with us have found that their hearts have opened to a greater experience of love as a result of RTT. From this more open-hearted place, they have been able to feel even closer to God.

We have worked with people who have a wide variety of beliefs and experiences, ranging from those who adhere to Eastern philosophies to Christians to atheists and just about everything in between. Some people believe in reincarnation and have direct experience with the spirit realm, while others do not. Whatever you believe or have previously experienced, RTT can still work for you.

For example, one of our clients, Claire, had what she believes to be a past life experience during RTT, yet it could just as easily be explained and processed as a symbolic waking dream. During her session, she felt like she was an African male being transported on a slave ship to America. She felt shackles around her wrists and ankles, reliving the experience of being this man in this place. In order to assist in Claire's healing, her facilitators treated the experience as if it were real and happening to her in the moment. Just as with soul retrieval, whether or not this was an actual past life that Claire experienced is irrelevant. It can easily be seen as a metaphor—a symbolic experience from her imagination, her psyche—that allowed her to release some inner trauma that may never be fully explained or understood. What's important is that she surrendered fully to the emotion and experience of it, trusting that the images came to her for a reason. And even more importantly, being fully open to the process allowed Claire to move her repressed energy and experience a state of inner calm.

At White Raven Center, we keep the concept of spirituality simple by merely acknowledging the presence and power of the light.

The RTT Process: Treatment for Trauma and PTSD

Our dedicated team of practitioners at White Raven Center support each participant's journey into the deepest and most uncharted parts of their being. The intent is to go to the source of the emotional pain. The act of feeling and moving stored emotional energy goes beyond casually sharing surface emotions or feelings.

To begin a session, the facilitator invites the participant to lie down on a padded mat, making sure the participant's spine is straight and legs are propped comfortably over a pillow to relieve tension in the lower back. A blindfold is placed over the eyes to create a sense of privacy and facilitate an easier journey "within." A light blanket is placed over the body for comfort and a further sense of privacy. If the client feels chilly, several blankets or a wool covering may be added. The goal is to make the person feel as physically comfortable as possible at the beginning of the session. The process of tapping into intense emotions will wake up body memories that may be extremely uncomfortable.

As the process begins, the individual simply closes his or her eyes and starts to breathe deeply, bringing attention and awareness to the breath as it goes in and out. It's really that simple, because the breath is the pathway to accessing emotions stored at a deep subconscious level. This natural and simple process requires nothing more than being present with the experience of the moment, and a willingness to surrender to that experience.

Proper and full breathing restores the body's natural capacity to heal itself. It also shifts conscious awareness from the ego mind to the heart. The breathwork breaks us from the perpetual thought processing that is the nature of the conscious mind. This shift in focus dissolves the control of the mind and opens us to connect with the truth in the body. Eckhart Tolle refers to this as tapping into the "pain body."

The breath is our life force. Notice how the belly rises and falls with each breath in a rhythmic pattern. As humans living in high-pressure societies, we have learned to disconnect from our natural way of breathing and, instead, breathe shallowly to numb ourselves from our painful emotions. As children we are natural trance inducers, and we discover early in life (depending on the level of trauma experienced) how to manipulate the breath, cut off the oxygen supply to our brains, and achieve a state of numbness. When we begin to center into deeper breathing during RTT, the mind often tries to distract us. We simply have to continue returning the focus to the breath. Facilitators can help participants to maintain that focus by reminding them to keep breathing. The facilitator might even audibly exhale with the participant, breathing with him or her to create a feeling of safety and quiet the mind. Once a breathing pattern is established the facilitator may offer a prayer that is in alignment with the participant's spiritual beliefs, asking for protection, guidance, and healing. At times, this may include the honoring of ancestral helpers.

The guided focus on breathing is used to teach the participant to tune in and listen to the body. We teach that the body never lies and, if we can just learn to listen to the body, we will know exactly where we need to do our work. When the mind becomes involved, we lose our connection with the body and its messages in the moment. As we come more fully into connection with the physical body, we learn to recognize where our conscious attention is focused and how we have learned to numb our pain by trying to figure things out with the intellect.

Rapid Transformation Therapy

As author Caroline Myss has said, "The soul always knows what to do to heal itself. The challenge is to silence the mind."

Our facilitator Toby Quinn explains it this way: "Ultimately, if we seek understanding with the conscious mind before the energy has moved, we are actually seeking to create an illusion of control. This is one way we avoid the experience of our feelings and simply 'write' a story that feels better." True transformation occurs when we relinquish control and surrender to the process.

We ask participants not to judge themselves for the mind's desire to control. It's simply a coping mechanism that most of us have learned to use to help us survive.

To benefit most from RTT, we enter into it with no expectations. We allow the truth of stored memories and emotions to rise to the surface without an agenda. Because of that allowing, our consciousness rises over the illusion of control and we connect with the wisdom of the universal mind, which we define as a pervasive source of intelligence and higher consciousness that goes well beyond the thinking mind.

As the session progresses, the participant will begin to tap into core emotional energy. When feelings start to emerge, the facilitator encourages the participant to keep breathing into those powerful feelings, to drop deeper into the feelings and stay with the process. Participants are encouraged to stay with the pain rather than run from it, in order to release and transform the pain and reach a state of inner peace.

Once stored emotional energy has been tapped, the process evolves in a manner that is unique to each individual. Many participants have vivid memories of past experiences of abuse or trauma. Facilitators support the participant by maintaining a safe space in which they can work with these memories and the emotions that surface. Participants may allow themselves to experience the deep feelings of sorrow, pain, grief, anger, rage, fear, and terror. By allowing for the full experience of these emotions, the blocked and stored energy in the body transforms.

Since the emotions can be intense, the feelings often do not come up all at once. Intense feelings are generally experienced in waves. The person might touch the feelings gently, then move deeper into the emotional-being state, staying with the intensity of the feelings as long as possible.

Facilitators assist the participant by helping identify the feelings. This is not about imposing ideas about what the individual is feeling, but about asking questions. For example, a facilitator might say, "I sense that you're feeling anger toward your mother. Is that what you're experiencing?" If the answer is yes, the facilitator would then encourage the person to sink deeper into the anger. This is done through continued focus on the breath, fully relaxing, and allowing the conscious awareness to shift from the mind to the heart center.

The most important aspect of the process is to acknowledge and stay with the feelings, whatever they are, without judgment. The deeper a person goes into the feeling state, the greater the progress of the treatment. Once the energies start to flow freely, the participant will begin to feel emotions that may never have been experienced before on a conscious level. When the individual stays with the feelings without judgment, following them to the core of his/her being, he/she no longer abandons the part of the self who has held onto those emotions. That is when soul retrieval is likely to occur as an organic part of the session.

At White Raven Center, there are several areas used for conducting healing sessions. We supply each with a variety of tools that can be used to either intensify or purge the feelings that have arisen. These include a plastic bat and a pad that participants can hit safely when they experience the emotion of rage, a wooden pole to grab or pull when tension needs to be created, a leather belt when the participant needs to imagine grabbing a belt away from an abusive caretaker, a baby doll wrapped in a bundle for times when the client is experiencing soul retrieval and integration, various sizes of pillows and stuffed animals both for holding and to create pressure, and old towels, rags, and sheets to tear up or shred as a way to release stress, tension, or even rage in the body. The RTT process is often long and explosive, yet the emotions expressed do not necessarily have to be "big" in order to be transformative. Huge shifts can occur in subtle and gentle ways that are almost imperceptible. We simply trust that the process unfolds in the way that it needs to unfold for the healing of each participant.

Kent, a young military veteran whose more detailed story you will read in a later chapter, has come to White Raven Center on three occasions to treat post-war PTSD. Kent likens the RTT process to massage therapy. "The massage therapist is working on you, and they hit a tight spot. Then, all of a sudden, they follow that tight spot to another place and work the whole area, and fifteen minutes later, you're feeling better and you can move better. So it's kind of like that—you find a knot of emotional energy, whatever that emotion may be, and you follow that down. It's got a little thread, and you follow that thread until it leads you to an area in yourself that needs to be healed or needs to be celebrated or needs to be brought out into the light."

Our client Tia says, "It's really cool when they have you lie down and put the blindfold on because you just go into yourself and let what comes up come up. Then, at the end of your session, it's like, 'Wow, I didn't realize that was in me' or 'Wow, that still bothers me?'"

The key—the main component of this work—is to reach a point where you can say, "I know that happened to me, and it used to bother me. And it isn't happening now, nor does it affect me anymore."

Who Is Ready for RTT?

"When we are no longer able to change a situation, we are challenged to change ourselves."

—Viktor E. Frankl

Defining RTT as a Method of Recovery

What I want you to know more than anything is that yes, you can heal yourself of traumas and hurts—even severe PTSD—without expensive treatments or dependency on prescriptions. You will need some help along the way, using the tools offered in this book, but you can do it if you're open to the experience.

There are many treatment methodologies available, and it is true that RTT is not for everyone. Again, it's an intense process, and you may not be ready for it yet. Safety factors must be considered when diving into deep realms of the emotional and mental bodies—"the pain body"—and you need to have someone with you while you do this work. That individual needs to understand the process and be able to handle the intensity of the emotions that could surface.

For this reason, it's best that you work with a trained therapist when processing with RTT. Eventually, when you have mastered the method, you might be able to process on your own as is the case for some of our clients. Please take care not to do this too soon. There is considerable benefit to allowing yourself to be vulnerable with human witness and allowing someone else to see your experience and your pain.

I always share the following with my clients in private sessions and at workshops, as a way of helping them see the power of human witness: "We were hurt at the hands of other human beings; therefore, in order to heal, we need to trust at least one other human being with the truth of our deepest suffering."

Our trust in other human beings is often shattered because our greatest pain originated in the presence of others. Floyd shares that by allowing others to witness his truth during RTT, he came to understand that what his family had told him about himself wasn't true. He wasn't stupid or worthless as he had always been told. As children, we give our power to adults and believe them. They're older, so we think they must know better. "Once the soul parts have had a chance to speak their truth and feel their pain, we can begin to forgive and let go of

Rapid Transformation Therapy

the need to stay in the victim story. We can then begin to take responsibility for our current experience," Floyd says.

At the end of this chapter, there is a self-assessment questionnaire that is designed to help you determine whether or not the time is right for you to experience the RTT process. Even if you discover that you aren't quite ready for deep processing, you can still read the book and learn how RTT works.

If you do locate a support person or facilitator to work with you through the process as it is presented in this book, you have the opportunity to access your inner wisdom and guidance, and to achieve a state of inner calm. Along the way, you will have the opportunity to learn crucial truths about the connections between trauma, soul loss, and physical, mental, and emotional imbalance—truths that can alter your perspective about yourself and your life.

I have divided the stories of our clients into chapters based on PTSD/trauma and abuse, addictions, caretaking behaviors and physical symptoms. These divisions have only been made in the interest of grouping experiences with some degree of similarity. What you will discover is that all emotional pain and the behaviors that result are due to some type of trauma.

(Note that I refer to people experiencing RTT as either "participants" or "clients." These terms are used interchangeably. Most RTT sessions last between ninety and one hundred and twenty minutes and some extend to four to five hours, so the stories in the book have been abbreviated for illustrative purposes.) Later in the book, I will offer tips for participants and practitioners who wish to try RTT on their own. The final chapter provides commentary on how each of us, as human beings who are committed and fully engaged in our own healing, can awaken our inner light and, in doing so, contribute to the healing of our world.

If you find that you are not yet ready to try RTT, working with a counselor or therapist in your community can often help you ready yourself for this deeper work. The main thing

Defining RTT as a Method of Recovery

required is a commitment to yourself and the desire to be more fully present in your life.

Self-Assessment of Readiness for RTT

Be sure to answer each question honestly, checking the box marked "Yes" or "No."

	Yes	No
• Am I tired of suffering and living in pain?	☐	☐
• Am I ready to surrender, allow my repressed emotions to surface, and share truth about the related event(s)?	☐	☐
• Am I ready to view my pain as a gift that will alleviate my suffering?	☐	☐
• Am I ready to allow others to witness my full truth and experience?	☐	☐
• Am I tired of feeling trapped in unhealthy cycles?	☐	☐
• Am I tired of feeling alone, empty, afraid and invisible?	☐	☐
• Am I ready to give up beliefs that no longer serve my higher good?	☐	☐
• Am I ready to give up my obsession with control?	☐	☐
• Am I ready to revisit painful or perhaps repressed memories of my most traumatic life events in order to heal them?	☐	☐

	Yes	No
• Am I ready to share my truth about shameful events that I have kept secret my entire life?	☐	☐
• Am I ready to give up the roles I have been programmed to play by my family and society if they do not reflect who I truly am?	☐	☐
• Am I ready to commit to my own self-care?	☐	☐
• Am I ready to forgive myself for my participation in my own suffering?	☐	☐
• Am I ready to stop judging myself and others?	☐	☐
• Am I ready to celebrate my life as opposed to merely existing?	☐	☐
• Am I open to change, relinquishing whatever does not serve me?	☐	☐
• Am I ready to embrace my inner truth, even if some of my loved ones may have trouble accept- ing that truth?	☐	☐
• Am I ready to stop caretaking others and to make caring for myself a number one priority?	☐	☐
• Am I ready to stop blaming others for all the negativity in my life?	☐	☐
• Am I ready to set myself free to consciously co-create and take responsibility for all that I manifest in my life?	☐	☐

Defining RTT as a Method of Recovery

These thought-provoking, perhaps even emotion-provoking, questions are intended to help you assess your readiness for engagement with RTT. There is no magic number that defines your readiness to commit to self-transformation. Only your inner wisdom can determine that, so use your answers to the questions as a means of self-discovery.

✦

Chapter 3

Understanding Emotional Energy—A Journey to the Core of Your Being

Emotions are something we all experience. They are an integral part of our shared human experience, together with body, mind and spirit. They are phenomena that allow us to gauge certain aspects of our existence in relation to others. In a way, emotions are messengers from the universe, speaking to our being and adding a rich dimension to our total human experience.

When we were children, most of us didn't have the experience of an adult caretaker assuring us that it is normal to have feelings. As a child, I don't remember the topics of "feelings" or "emotions" ever being discussed. I do remember feeling terrified when my father had outbursts of anger. I also remember being shamed or punished when I had my own angry outbursts. This was confusing to me. I was not guided to understand that my feelings were valid and that I had the right to express them. Since no one communicated otherwise, I assumed and adopted a core belief that there must be something wrong with me. As a result, I became insecure and withheld expressing my truth to others. In working with clients for more than thirty-five years, I have come to understand that this is a common experience.

As children, most of us learn about feelings by guessing, ignoring, or stuffing them down. How our adult caretakers express anger is generally how we learn to express anger. How they express love is how we learn to express it, and so on. To put an end to a discussion with children, adults commonly use the phrase "because I told you so," leaving the child to guess at the real reasoning.

Unfortunately, society hasn't done any better as a model where emotions are concerned. Society tells us it's more acceptable to express what we consider "positive" or "feel-good" emotions than "negative" or "feel-bad" emotions. We're conditioned to apply value judgments and meanings to our feelings. Some emotions are considered to be strong, some are weak, some are dangerous, and some are unacceptable.

The feelings associated with emotions should not be confused with the feelings we experience at an intuitive level. Intuitive feelings and emotional feelings are vastly different. Intuitive feelings guide us and tap our wisdom and keen sense of knowingness. Emotional feelings encompass the range of sensations we attribute to anger, sadness, guilt, shame, loneliness, fear and grief or, on the other end of the continuum, joy, happiness, gratitude and love. Both emotional feelings and intuitive feelings play a role in guiding us to a place where we raise our vibration and can experience states of calmness, contentment, ecstasy, bliss and inner peace. Intuitive feelings tell us to allow for the presence and release of emotional feelings. In doing so, they work together to aid in our actualization of healing and raising our vibration.

A Difference in Vibration

Emotions vibrate at different frequencies depending on which feeling a particular emotion is charged with. For example, if I become angry and do not express that anger in some appropriate way, I will store a low vibrational energy in my body. I will have swallowed a heavy energy form. If I am experiencing a deep sense of gratitude I vibrate at a high-energy frequency, which promotes the natural flow of energy in my body. In this case, no concentrated blocks of energy are created, and nothing is stored in the body; feelings and emotions simply flow through my being with ease.

Most of the emotions stuck in the body are what we have decided are undesirable feelings and resentments. These stuck energies can lead to emotional, psychological and physical illness, causing all sorts of suffering. We end up disconnected from who we really are, and we feel a sense of emptiness and a lack of personal power over our own lives.

The disconnect happens because we deny our "feel-bad" emotions, stuff them down, and pretend they don't exist. We become disconnected from the parts of ourselves that feel the emotions we want to pretend away. In this way, we abandon a part of the self. And most of us do this so automatically that we aren't even aware of it.

Since we apply judgments to our emotions, the mind struggles to make sense of the coexistence of conflicting feelings. You might love your mother, yet a part of you might also hate her. Since your mind judges the hatred, you suppress it. On some level, you might feel that the hatred or anger threatens the love you also feel. In actuality, that hatred will only threaten your love *because* you suppress it. When you do so, it's likely to come out in covert ways that could be destructive to your relationship with your mother. If, on the other hand, you "process" those feelings of hatred and anger—inviting the hatred to come out fully in a healthy, therapeutic environment—you release it and strengthen your love for your mother, as well as your ability to express that love without fear or condition, without the hatred or anger "leaking" out in your behavior or words.

Emotions are feedback from our choices and perspective. We create them, and they aren't right or wrong. If we express our emotions in a way that hurts someone else, we could perhaps apply "right" or "wrong" judgments to the *actions* we have taken. However, pretending certain emotions don't exist because we don't like them creates a host of behaviors that are destructive to the self and relationships. As human beings, we are entitled to experience our full range of emotions—whatever they are. Part of RTT is becoming conscious of when we are hurting others by inappropriately blasting them with our feelings, then learning to share truth without projecting the intense energy of our emotions onto others.

At the White Raven Center, when we talk about the phenomenon of "not being in my body," we are referring to two things: The process of numbing ourselves so that we do not have to feel painful emotions, and the habit of focusing our attention on anything other than what is happening in our bodies in the present moment. This does not necessarily mean the person has had an "out of body experience." As we discussed in the last chapter, when we deny our feelings repeatedly, we unconsciously disengage from our bodies. We tune out our experience to such a degree that we may even not feel a lot of the body's sensations.

Another common experience that relates to "not being in my body" is when our thoughts are so engaged in future events that we project ourselves out of present space and time. Some people are so disconnected from their bodies that they may even black out for a period of time during the processing session.

Through RTT, we teach people to reconnect with their bodies. This enhances each person's ability to connect more fully with his or her true feelings. At times, clients may "disconnect" right in the middle of a processing session, because the habit of escaping the body's feelings is just so deeply ingrained. Over time, they learn to catch themselves disconnecting and "come back" so that they can stay fully connected to their being. They do that by focusing on their breath—the pathway back into the body.

One of our clients, Cathy, illustrates how this disconnect occurs. She often had trouble catching her breath in the mornings after awakening. Before coming to White Raven Center she tended to breathe very shallowly, and she had to work to stay in her body during her emotional processing sessions. "I really controlled my breathing down to repress my anxiety," she says. "I learned that as soon as I started breathing, I started feeling; and as soon as I started feeling, I stepped out of my body in a way. I dissociated and went far enough away that it was difficult for me to hear the facilitators talk. They would continue to talk to me and reassure me, and I would come back and work a little bit. Then I would get scared again and step away. To locate feelings, you have to come back in your body. Over a period of probably six months of practicing, I came to realize on a deep level that I was safe. Then I stopped disappearing out of my body like that." Cathy credits RTT with teaching her how to breathe from her diaphragm.

We are meant to breathe from our diaphragms, remain in our bodies, and stay present in the moment of now. As Eckhart Tolle tells us in his book *A New Earth*, "Who you are cannot be defined through thinking or mental labels or definitions because it's beyond that. It is the very sense of being, or presence, that is there when you become conscious of the present moment. In essence, you and what we call the present moment are, at the deepest level, one."

What Are Emotions?

Your emotions are messengers from the universe, speaking to your being and adding a rich dimension to your total human experience. They are phenomena that allow you to gauge certain aspects of your existence in relation to others. They're energy forms, as are all things in this universe. They flow through you, and *you are not your emotions*. Let me say that again: You are *not* your emotions. We *experience* emotions; we *are* not emotions.

We tend to say "I am sad" instead of "I feel sad," yet the second expression is the accurate one. When we identify emotional energy forms as part of ourselves, instead of allowing them to move through our bodies, they create blocks in the natural flow and rhythm of the body's energy system. Eventually, these stuck energies of emotion manifest in neuroses, phobias, and various forms of disease or other physical ailments.

At times, part of our human experience is to endure immense emotional pain and suffering. How much repressed emotional energy we have stored relates to the extent of trauma and oppression we have experienced. People who have been victims of repeated trauma without the opportunity to heal are likely to have stored an abundant supply of emotional energy. This means that to some degree, they are numb or partially frozen emotionally. The degree to which we block our feelings of pain is equivalent to the degree to which we block our feelings of joy.

At White Raven Center, I routinely remind clients that "feeling is healing." To block feeling is to promote increased suffering. In order to release the pain in our lives, we must first be willing to allow for its existence. Through the allowing, we give ourselves the opportunity to discharge the emotion.

When we stop seeing feelings as who we are and begin to see them instead as teachers, messengers, and allies on our path to wholeness, we are able to feel them, fully release the charge they create in our body, and reclaim our power over the suffering caused by repressed emotions.

Some participants have voiced concern that expressing negative emotions results in "putting negative energy out there into the universe." If you express hatred toward your mother even when she isn't around to hear it, will she be energetically harmed by your emotions?

When you express yourself in a safe environment that is geared toward your own healing, the intention is positive and loving. Your intention is not to hurt anyone, even if you are screaming profanities at your mother in your RTT processing session. This release of energy is not harmful to your mother, because you are actually transmuting the energy into a lighter form. The dense energy of anger, hate and rage is transformed at the level of your heart center and becomes the energy of acceptance and gratitude. This raising of your energetic vibration positively affects all of the beings whose lives you touch.

Emotional Triggers

"Traumatic symptoms are not caused by the 'triggering' event itself. They stem from the frozen residue of energy that has not been resolved and discharged; this residue remains trapped in the nervous system where it can wreak havoc on our bodies and spirits."

—Peter A. Levine[2]

---

[2] Levine, Waking the Tiger, 19.

Storing emotional energy *requires* a lot of energy—so many of us waste considerable energy, without ever knowing it at a conscious level, by holding onto old, repressed feelings. Even when we hold onto our negative emotions and actively hold them back from our own awareness, they are still there in the body or psyche, ready to be triggered at any moment. "Triggering" is what happens when some person, place, event, smell or situation activates repressed emotional energy that's stored in your being. When triggered, you feel that charge of energy running through your body.

Many of us are "emotional reactors." Some people might be considered "super-sensitive" or "touchy." The degree to which someone is an emotional reactor in his or her life is directly proportionate to the amount of energy that is being suppressed within. It's natural, of course, to feel anger when someone "pushes our buttons," and the tendency is to blame the other person. But when we have powerful emotional reactions, we're actually reacting from those stored emotional energies rather than what appears to be transpiring at face value. This is what it means to be emotionally triggered. Healing requires that we acknowledge that our emotions and feelings are never about the other person, but are instead about ourselves.

When we become triggered we may project our inner trauma onto a situation, another person, or a group of people. We may try to make someone else responsible for what *we're* feeling. Yes, someone else may have harmed us. Ultimately, however, we are responsible for our feelings about what happened. We all do this at times—yet the more we become aware of our projections, the healthier and happier we can be. When we use an emotional trigger as an opportunity to heal instead of to blame, we contribute to the wellness of ourselves and those around us.

How Projections Trigger Us

Often, our parents and caretakers unconsciously project their own childhood trauma onto us as children. When we're small we unwittingly trigger their own childhood experiences, especially when we try to get their attention. The adults then feel the need to respond in controlling ways. They are not conscious of their behavior and how it affects us as children. Their obsession with control is a byproduct of *their* own repressed pain and soul loss.

Our behavior as children is generally a response to a lack of presence and consciousness on the part of the parent or guardian. Their lack of presence and consciousness is, in turn, because no one was ever present for them. And the vicious cycle continues: perceived abandonment, neglect, and all forms of abuse are projected back and forth between generations and between people in all forms of relationships and circumstances.

Let's say John's father often told him that he would never amount to anything. "You can't do anything right," John's father said repeatedly, probably because he'd heard the same thing from his own dad.

As an adult, John is insecure and pretends that he's confident. He may mask his insecurities with the expression of anger. In fact, he isn't even aware of his underlying insecurity. Instead, John projects his insecurity out toward others. As a result, he's easily angered (i.e., easily triggered) about the possibility of being criticized. The minute anyone says anything that remotely sounds like criticism, John projects the voice of his father's judgment onto the other person and reacts. John is unconsciously searching for that judgment, through even a subtle look or a slight comment, because he expects it.

There are times when John simply imagines that someone else is criticizing him, even though that person has never said a word. John may be imagining the criticism entirely—it might not even exist. How many lost relationships and incidents of violence are a result of projection like John's, every day around the world? How many guns have been fired because of this very kind of projection? More than we can count. That's how powerful and potentially damaging projection can be.

When left untreated, PTSD directs our life experience as if we are living from the parts of ourselves that have been hurt. We see the world through the lens of our past traumatic life events, and our reactions are often a direct result of this unresolved trauma. When we are disconnected from our feelings and our true inner selves, we are driven by our emotions without ever realizing it. We live our lives on automatic pilot and in defensive mode, poised and ready to fight battles that have nothing to do with what we are experiencing in the present moment. As a result, we deny ourselves the gift of taking action by choice.

When the trauma is treated, however, we can break the destructive cycle of intergenerational trauma and begin to make conscious choices that are healthy for ourselves and our relationships with others. We take back our ability to act by choice in the present (instead of continually reacting to old traumas), and begin to create a life of our own. We succeed in diminishing the power of stored emotional energy. We are no longer emotional reactors; we become witnesses to our own lives and to the lives of others.

Many people attempt to avoid the intense feelings that arise when triggered energies are activated. They simply rid themselves of the marriage, the children, the job, or whatever other person or circumstance has triggered those emotional wounds and lost soul parts. Running away from the triggers doesn't solve the problem, because the unresolved wounds come along for the ride. Those triggers actually present us with the opportunity to heal and restore our lives to a place of balance.

Once we release the energy of our unresolved feelings, we cleanse our bodies of the toxicity generated by stored emotions of anger, rage, guilt, shame, grief, hate and fear. When those heavy energies transform, the emotional trigger evaporates; the ability to observe without emotional reaction is renewed. When we see the world from a place of presence and observation, there is no problem. We no longer react impulsively to emotional triggers.

As we release the anger that we feel toward others and whatever blame we carry within, we take back responsibility for our own reactions and emotions. We diminish the need to project, and we become more aware of our tendency to do so. As the emotions come up to the surface where we can see and know them, we gain clarity about how we have projected those feelings onto others. We start to catch ourselves and pull back the projections before our emotions erupt. This is not the same as stuffing feelings down. It's an awareness of the true source of our feelings and a *choice* to express ourselves in a healthy way.

Speaking Truth

Truth is a powerful healer. Speaking truth to another human being, with the added dimension of emotional truth, is powerful medicine for the soul.

Why do we need to "re-experience" traumas in order to heal them? When you first experience a trauma, you are entrenched in the pain of the experience. When you re-experience it in the therapeutic atmosphere, you are observing or witnessing it from a place of awareness. This is how healing occurs. RTT doesn't require that you *fully* re-experience all of the pain you felt when the trauma took place. Facilitators need to stay aware of this and not allow a participant to stay locked into an experience of the wounding for too long. The process is about acknowledging what occurred so that it can be healed and let go. This might involve speaking a truth that the individual was unable to speak during the initial trauma.

The experience of allowing your traumatized parts to speak truth is a necessary aspect of the healing process. This piece is critical because it frees the hurt parts of your self from bondage to the traumatic event. For example, when our client Angie first started in treatment with us, she had trouble swallowing and complained of a lump in her throat. She was always clearing her throat and had been to numerous specialists only to be told "nothing is wrong."

Once Angie was able to speak her full truth in her initial RTT processes, all of the energy in her throat cleared. The sensation of the lump dissolved, and she felt the victim energy evaporate. As a child, her parents had constantly yelled at her, saying that she was stupid and should "keep quiet." She had a core belief that she had no right to speak truth. Through RTT, Angie was able to courageously stand up for herself and give voice to the parts that previously felt unworthy and invisible.

When we experience traumatic events or recurrent instances of disappointment, frustration or judgment from others at any age, we feel like victims to circumstances beyond our control. When trust is broken at thehandsof otherhumanbeings, we stop trusting others and ourselves. The pattern of broken trust repeatedly plays out in our lives. We discover that we attract people who are not trustworthy. We may also become vulnerable as we fear and question everything and doubt our own inner knowingness. We can be easily persuaded by others and emotionally invest in the agreement that we have no truth of our own.

As children, when we ask questions that go unanswered or when we're told to be quiet, we lose our voices in a sense—we lose the opportunity to speak our truth. The ability to express ourselves is often taken away at such an early age that we have no real experience of expressing ourselves at all. We aren't allowed to say what we truly feel, so our real emotions go into hiding and come out in covert ways. And, just as I felt when I was a child, we believe that something is wrong with us. As a result, negative self- talk explodes and can consume us over the course of a lifetime. Author Louise Hay has estimated that the average person repeats negative self-talk up to 60,000 times a day.

When mental and emotional pressures become too much for us as children, our feeling parts—hope, innocence, courage, determination, faith, trust, playfulness and curiosity—fade into the background and only surface when we are in a loving, safe and nurturing environment. An example of this is when a child shuts down in his parents' home but transforms into an open, secure, and flourishing child when visiting loving grandparents.

As children, we also often absorb the suppressed emotions of our parents and unconsciously act them out. For example, if our parents are angry but not expressing it, we might have a tantrum. It's a way of releasing the tension without having any idea that is what we are doing. If our parents react by punishing us for releasing tension the only way we know how, it becomes a very confusing predicament.

Most children react to losing their voice of truth by either becoming extremely introverted or acutely reactive. The reactive child is often scolded for "acting out." It's a type of "bleeding" of the true but hidden emotions—the voice of truth—within the child. Reactive children may turn into bullies, while children who respond by becoming timid are generally those who are bullied. Either way, the cause is suppressed emotional trauma as a result of the child's inability to speak his or her truth.

It is a sad reality that society often perpetuates and reinforces the isolation of the introverted child, while at the same time being punitive, even abusive, toward the reactive, acting-out child, further damaging the souls in both cases. On the introverted side of the spectrum, the child may be too shy to speak up in classroom, social or family settings, so they are quickly overlooked by the adults and other children around them. This reinforces their sense of low self-worth and extreme introversion.

In Floyd's Alaska Native culture, he was taught that listening and observing was a sign of respect. A child was not to speak up unless directly asked a question. Historically, this has been misinterpreted by the dominant society as stupidity, ignorance and apathy, which has further silenced and inhibited many children's growth and self-esteem.

On the other hand, a child who rebels repeatedly and acts out may receive disciplinary action in school, the community, and the family, without any opportunity for healing. This punitive treatment of children may lead to bullying and other aggressive behaviors. Although Floyd himself was only marginally rebellious, he witnessed other young men excel at breaking into businesses to steal and engage in other criminal acts. This is a prime example of how using physical "discipline" as a way of controlling young people, together with psychological abuse and neglect, perpetuates unhealthy behaviors instead of resolving them.

Regardless of where a child falls on the reactivity/introversion spectrum, if he or she is living in a situation that is in any way traumatic, he/she will become hypervigilant as a way of surviving. It's important to note that we are not talking about what happens in a healthy, "normal" household in which family roles are fluid and characterized by openness, honesty, flexibility, creativity and spontaneity. We are talking about families who take sides, participate in bashing others, and make their children keep secrets. To survive such circumstances, children learn to focus on pleasing the adults around them so that they can continue to safely navigate what is coming next. This is what we mean by hypervigilance.

What RTT does is give our inner children back their voices. By allowing these young parts of ourselves to *finally* say what they need to say, healing can take place and soul retrieval does occur. From an adult perspective, during the process of RTT, we give our inner children a mature vocabulary and awareness so that the expression is beyond what a child might have been able to articulate.

The images that come up during RTT can be childhood memories, possible past-life memories like Claire's experience on a slave ship, or they can be completely new experiences. We trust the images that come to a client during RTT and follow those images where they lead. The intention is healing, so the images are there for that purpose—even if they don't always make rational sense.

For example, in an RTT session one of our clients, Bertha, spoke directly to the parents who constantly left her alone from infancy up until age seven (while they were out drinking alcohol). In her mind's eye, Bertha let her parents witness how terrified she was. "It wasn't right when you left me alone. I was barely older than a baby! I was terrified. I didn't know how to take care of myself! How could you leave me like that?"

Conversations like Bertha's are necessary to bring closure to the traumatic events in our lives. By speaking truth, we set ourselves free and experience inner peace. For some, the process is gradual and requires multiple sessions; for others, it happens amazingly fast. Either way, completing the healing process brings us to a place where we are no longer affected by the past trauma. We can honestly say, "It did happen, and it is not happening now." The end result of speaking truth is freedom. As we speak truth, we dissolve the contracts and agreements that no longer serve us. We come to a place of acceptance that our parents did to us what was done to them. As Floyd puts it, "I no longer need my parents to love me—because I love me."

"Soul loss is a spiritual illness that causes emotional
and physical disease. The concept of soul
loss involves losing crucial parts of ourselves that provide
us with life and vitality. These parts get lost through
trauma, and who has suffered the most trauma
but the children who live inside us?"

—Sandra Ingerman

Chapter 4

Participatory Soul Retrieval

When I met Amy in 1994—while I was an itinerant mental health worker for one of Alaska's rural communities—her breathing was shallow and she slouched in her chair, looking fatigued to the point of exhaustion. Her eyes were sunken and surrounded by deep, dark circles, and the tone and quality of her voice sounded like someone who had given up on life. She seemed far away from her body, as if she were ready to die, and I intuitively felt a profound sense of emptiness within her.

I soon found out that Amy had been barely eating, and she had ceased taking care of her six-year-old daughter. As her story unfolded over the course of our sessions, recurring themes of self-criticism, self-doubt, self-sacrifice, and self-hatred emerged.

I was both fascinated and puzzled by Amy's case, so I consulted with a trusted colleague, who said that it sounded to her as though Amy was suffering from "soul loss." I wasn't familiar with the condition, so my colleague enlightened me. When I heard the description, it fit with my observations of Amy's symptoms. After gentle inquiry during a later session with Amy, I discovered that she herself attributed her condition to soul loss. She was aware that she was struggling for survival, and had already connected her challenges to a time when she felt that she had consciously given up a part of her own soul.

She shared with me that at the age of sixteen, she began dating a significantly older man. Her mother encouraged the relationship as a way of relieving herself of responsibility for her daughter's care. Unfortunately, Amy soon discovered that the man was manipulative and controlling. He was also secretly participating in an underground cult, and he groomed Amy to accept its teachings. Out of fear for her life, she found herself participating in sacrificial rituals.

Even though she was eventually able to escape the grip of the man and the cult, Amy continued to live in a state of fear. Now, after many years of working with clients who have experienced trauma, I know that Amy was in shock and suffering from PTSD. Amy also had a secret that she had never told anyone; yet, she chose to share it with me. She knew the precise day, time, and place when she relinquished a part of her soul.

My colleague suggested that Amy might need a healing methodology called "soul retrieval," and she recommended a reliable shamanic practitioner to do that work. Amy jumped at the opportunity and elected to travel to experience the soul retrieval process. When she returned to Alaska and shared her experience with me, I was struck by the fact that the process had been done for her. She had not been an active participant in the retrieval.

Amy had been instructed not to journey into an altered (hypnotic/meditative) state of reality along with the shamanic practitioner. She stayed present and fully awake while the practitioner traveled into the spirit world to retrieve Amy's lost soul parts and return them to her. (By "traveled" we mean a non-physical form of travel, in which the shaman journeys to another realm of reality in spirit form.)

Amy did experience healing as a result of her session, and I was extremely grateful for that. Still, the lack of direct participation in her own healing journey bothered me, perhaps because my social work training places great emphasis on practicing and teaching techniques that fully engage and empower clients to heal themselves. I felt intuitively guided to create a ritual for Amy to perform each day, a way of actively welcoming her soul parts back home.

She would light a candle, express thanks for her healing, and speak truthfully to herself in the mirror. Amy reassured her returned soul parts that her physical body had become a safe place. As a result, she discovered pangs of hunger in her body and reconnected to the foods she once loved. She began to engage in other soul-nurturing activities, too. When she was sixteen, Amy had loved to weave friendship bracelets. She resurrected this craft and began teaching her daughter how to make the bracelets.

What Amy did was "anchor" the soul parts in her body so that soul loss would be less likely to recur. We discuss this, and other ways of maintaining the benefits of RTT despite life's challenges, in chapter 10. In Amy's case, her ritual served a dual purpose. She also reconnected and bonded with her daughter. She began to shift out of the soul loss, emptiness and depression she had been suffering from. Amy was able to nurture her physical body and soul, and she became an active participant in her daughter's care once again.

Amy and I continued our work together for a number of months, exploring previously repressed traumatic events from her childhood. She came to recognize her inherent value in the world and became an active volunteer in her daughter's school. Her husband supported her healing journey, and their relationship improved dramatically. He had been terrified of losing his wife, so he was overwhelmed with gratitude for the positive changes he witnessed in her.

Amy became present within herself, and discovered that she had the strength to continue on a path of healthy and soul-nurturing life choices. By reconnecting to the previously fragmented parts of her own soul, she turned the corner and awakened to being fully engaged in life. I was in awe as I watched her transformation, and I had a thirst to learn more about soul retrieval, the nature of the soul, and its role in healing.

Soul Retrieval Methodology

It was clear that traditional Western treatment methods had not been enough to serve Amy, and I saw that the soul retrieval had indeed helped to facilitate her desired healing. I set out to learn more about soul retrieval, starting by reading *The Way of the Shaman* by Michael Harner. His book referred me to Sandra Ingerman's book *Soul Retrieval*. Both were instrumental in expanding my awareness of alternative types of healing work that are conducted in non-ordinary reality, including soul retrieval. I learned that the practice of reclaiming lost parts of our souls has traditionally been performed by indigenous shamans and, more recently, by shamanic practitioners.

In many indigenous cultures, there are spiritual healers known as medicine men or women, tribal doctors, sleep doctors, or shamans. These are similar to some of the elders I met in the Alaska Native villages where I began my social work experience.

Mircea Eliade, author of *Shamanism: Archaic Techniques of Ecstasy*, describes a shaman as a person who makes a journey in an altered state of consciousness outside of time and space.[3] Sandra Ingerman states that through such journeys, a shaman retrieves aid and information to help a patient, family member, friend or community.[4]

---

[3] Mircea Eliade, Shamanism: Archaic Techniques of Ecstasy, (Princeton Uni- versity Press, 1951).
[4] Sandra Ingerman, Soul Retrieval: Mending the Fragmented Self (HarperOne, 1991), 1.

I was drawn to this phenomenon of journeying into non-ordinary reality and curious about how it might help me aid in the healing of my clients' traumatic life events. Approximately two years after working with Amy, I had the opportunity to witness a traditional form of soul retrieval at an intensive training session I attended in California.

While lying on the floor next to the client, the teacher dropped into an altered state of consciousness with the help of a recorded drumming tape. She instructed the client to stay present in a fully awakened state and not to journey with her into an altered state. When the special basket used to carry the soul part home started shaking, it signaled that the teacher had been successful in retrieving a soul part for the client. Soon after this, she sat up and blew the soul essence into the top of the client's head and the heart center.

This soul retrieval practice followed the customs traditionally used among tribes across the globe, although the shaman might use rattles, trance-inducing herbs, or a skin drum instead of a drumming tape, and the soul retrieval might include blowing vital essence back into the participant's body through the bottoms of the feet, as well as through the crown and heart centers. In her book *Soul Retrieval*, Ingerman writes that "My next job is to bring these parts back from non-ordinary reality to ordinary reality by visualizing and feeling them with me. I slowly and firmly hold them to my heart, and then I physically get up and kneel next to my client. I cup my hands over my client's 'heart center' and deliberately blow the soul parts through my hands into the body, visualizing them entering into the entire body."[5]

---

[5] Ibid, 74.

Core Emotions Ignite the Soul Retrieval Process

Prior to witnessing soul retrieval methods, I began to make a connection between deep core emotional processing and the return of soul parts. I repeatedly observed what seemed to be a natural return of soul parts when clients allowed for deep emotional release and expression. Floyd was concurrently experiencing the same phenomenon in his work with clients, and we were both fascinated by the shifts that occurred.

I deeply honor the wisdom keepers of our tribal cultures, and I have profound respect for the ancient indigenous method of soul retrieval. Nevertheless, I could not help but wonder if it would be more empowering to retrieve lost parts of our own souls rather than have a practitioner do it for us. Thus was born what I have referred to for almost two decades as participatory soul retrieval.

What Is the Soul?

"Sigmund Freud described the mind as functioning on different levels. Among them is what is called the unconscious mind, of which we are not aware, by definition, but which stores all our experience and directs us to act as we do, think as we do, respond as we do, feel as we do. Only by accessing the unconscious, he saw, can we learn who we are and, with that knowledge, be able to heal. Some people have written that this is what the soul is—Freud's unconscious."

—Brian Weiss[6]

---

[6] Brian L. Weiss, Same Soul, Many Bodies: Discover the Healing Power of Fu- ture Lives through Progression Therapy, (Free Press, 2004), 7

Participatory Soul Retrieval

My first direct experience of witnessing the soul occurred while in a deep processing session of my own, when I experienced a vision of two souls that were somehow connected to me. I recognized that the souls were not complete or whole. I had a knowingness that what I was seeing was only part of these two beings. I saw billions, perhaps trillions, of tiny particles of light. It was like looking up at the Milky Way on a clear night. That is the closest I can come to describing the depth and expansiveness of my experience. Yet, it was as clear to me as seeing another person across the room.

Floyd had a similar experience during one of his deep healing sessions. He looked down at his arms and hands and saw his body as a luminous, silvery, shimmering form. He was filled with euphoria and joy and in awe, aware that he was seeing his true soul essence.

The soul is impossible to see with the naked eye or even with a high-powered microscope. However, quantum physicists tell us that there is significant scientific evidence of the existence of the human soul, and more evidence has been captured with advanced bioelectrographic cameras. It is also true that 99.999 percent of all that exists in the universe occurs in the unseen world. Physicists tell us that this same percentage of "empty space" makes up the majority of the human body.

According to the *Oxford English Dictionary*, the soul is "the principle of intelligence, thought, or action in a person, typically regarded as an entity distinct from the body."[7] It consists of the spiritual parts in contrast to the physical. My personal concept of the soul is that it's made up of tiny particles of light, and these particles join together with consciousness to make up the soul's essence. The soul can be considered our essential or vital life force. Deepak Chopra defines the soul

---

[7] Oxford English Dictionary, http://www.oed.com/view/Entry/185083?rskey=i AaX6U&result=1#eid, accessed 1 Dec. 2014.

as your core consciousness, the ground of your being.[8] He also proclaims that "to be disconnected from your soul is the ultimate disease."[9] My experience substantiates this as truth. We come into a physical body to have a human experience. Therefore, the rightful home of the soul for this part of our journey is within the body. We cannot thrive without this vital essence intact. When all of our soul parts are present in our bodies we feel fully connected, enjoying a sense of calm and communion with our true selves.

Signs and Symptoms of Soul Loss

People all over the world are not aware that many of our life challenges and uncomfortable symptoms are indicators of soul loss. Society's programming has us chasing "happiness" that we are convinced is located outside of ourselves in another person, job, accomplishment, or place. No matter how much we excel in certain areas of our lives, we may find ourselves wondering: "Why do I feel empty inside? Why is there always a longing for something more? Why do I react to certain people and situations as if controlled by some unseen force? Why do I sometimes feel like I'm disconnected from or out of my body?" In numerous cases, the answers to these questions lie in the phenomenon of soul loss.

Some common diagnostic signs of soul loss include:
- Chronic depression
- Anxiety state as a norm
- Habitual worry

---

[8] Deepak Chopra, "Ask Deepak," http://www.deepakchopra.com/video/view/210/ask_deepak_what_is_the_soul, accessed 1 Dec. 2014.
[9] Deepak Chopra, Publishers Weekly, "Why I Write," http://www.publisher- sweekly.com/pw/by-topic/authors/interviews/article/1657-why-i-write-deep- ak-chopra.html, accessed 1 Dec. 2014.

- Insomnia
- Feeling stuck in a victim role
- Loss of energy
- Loss of interest in things once enjoyed
- Desire to sleep all the time
- Prolonged feelings of loneliness and apathy
- Difficulty remembering past traumas
- Feeling that no one cares
- Feeling invisible
- Terror at speaking in front of a group
- Feeling empty inside

Physical symptoms are also sometimes an indication of soul loss, such as:
- Chronic illness and fatigue
- Body pain that has no clear explanation
- Extreme weight gain or loss
- Stomach issues
- Heart problems
- Difficulty breathing

Self-destructive patterns and behaviors of many kinds, including addictions, can be attributed to soul loss. Most of us aren't aware of the prevalence of soul loss and how much it affects our well-being.

If you'd like another tool for evaluating yourself, Sandra Ingerman's book *Soul Retrieval* contains an excellent checklist of symptoms attributed to soul loss on pages 22 and 23.

Causes of Soul Loss

Indigenous tribes across the globe have long understood that traumatic life events frequently resulted in some form of fragmentation of the soul or separation from it. Simply put, trauma shocks the system and produces soul loss. In *Soul Retrieval,* Sandra Ingerman tells us that whenever we experience trauma, a part of our vital essence or soul separates from us in order to escape the full impact of the pain, allowing you to survive what might otherwise be unsurvivable: "In ancient times, loss of our vital essence was attributed to the soul being frightened away, straying or being stolen. Today we often find soul loss as a result of such traumas as incest, abuse, loss of a loved one, surgery, accidents, illness, miscarriage, abortion, the stress of combat and addiction."

The effect of traumatic events on the soul can't be minimized, measured, or compared with the experiences of others. The bottom line is that any time the soul experiences trauma—regardless of the age or stage of life, whether in this lifetime or in a past lifetime—parts of the soul flee to escape the emotional pain. This disconnect can occur in a wide variety of ways and for an endless number of reasons. In my experience, all traumatic experiences that are left unprocessed and untreated result in some form of soul loss.

Emotional Overwhelm and Soul Loss

We are born with pure and innocent souls. As babies and young children we are givers of unconditional love, and we assume that this love will be reciprocated by our parents or other caretakers. We expect that those we love will love us in return, and we feel shocked when this energy of love is not available to us. The pain and betrayal of this shock become far too intense for us to handle, so we experience both sensory and emotional overwhelm that results in the departure of parts of the soul. To survive, we disconnect. When parts of our souls leave our bodies, it's an unconscious act of self-preservation.

Soul loss can happen at any age. Whenever we experience or observe a tragedy or traumatic event that's beyond our scope of tolerance, we "check out." It's too much. In shock, parts of our souls leave our bodies. Some people lost parts of their souls on 9/11, for example—the people who were in the World Trade Center or waiting for loved ones to come home from the towers or responding to calls for help.

This tragedy generated sensory overwhelm. The effects on each person varied, with some experiencing anxiety, fear, emptiness, rage, and depression—all symptoms that are connected to soul loss.

How Participatory Soul Retrieval Works

During one of her participatory soul retrieval sessions, my client Tia—who was forty-three years old at the time—saw herself in her mind's eye as a five-year-old child, lying on her bed while her mother's boyfriend sexually abused her. She had a conscious memory of multiple instances of abuse, which included violence as well as sexual molestation. As Tia experienced the memory during the session, she sensed her soul leaving her body and floating above her near the ceiling. Tia recognized that this phenomenon occurred frequently throughout her childhood as a means of surviving the terrifying episodes of abuse. Her experience depicts vividly how soul loss occurs in the moment of trauma.

At first, Tia didn't understand the concept of bringing a soul part "home." "To me, home was your house," she says.

Then, during the session just mentioned, I encouraged Tia's higher self to allow the five-year-old to speak. Within moments of my suggestion, I heard the deeply hurt voice of a five-year-old scolding someone for abandoning her. "Why did you leave me? You left me alone! Why do you hate me? I'm so scared. Please help me."

Tia's adult voice responded with, "I'm really sorry. I didn't mean to hurt you. I didn't know what I was doing. I wasn't taught how to love you and protect you. I love you."

Tia's five-year-old voice returned, crying and sharing intense fear. "How do I know you won't leave me out here again?"

The adult Tia cried as she shared her strong desire for her five- year-old soul part to allow for the nurturing, love and acceptance of her adult self. "Please come home. Please let me love you. Please forgive me." At this point, adult Tia told me that in her mind's eye she could see her five-year-old self reaching out, wanting to be held. As Tia envisioned herself holding this little girl version of herself, she continued speaking to that little girl, telling her that she was loved and it was time to come home. This allowed the process of integration to occur.

Often, at this moment in a session, the facilitator will place a pillow, stuffed animal, or baby doll in the client's arms to represent a physical manifestation of the soul part. Doing so can trigger a powerful reaction of deep gratitude and joy.

"When I held her, it was like we became one," Tia says. "It was a warm feeling. As I was hugging her she kind of melted into me, and we merged."

After her first soul retrieval, Tia says, "I felt like I finally understood what it meant to be home, what it meant to be inside myself and feel like I belong in my body. I belonged in my skin, and I was home. Home was where I felt loved—not just by other people, but loved by myself." Prior to RTT, Tia says the concept of self-love was foreign to her. She only understood that you could love other people.

Soul retrieval is often euphoric for Tia, and she feels tingly all over—a happy, warm feeling, leaving her more self-assured, alive, and present in her body. At times, she feels like she's floating. "Everything's brighter, and it's like my hearing improves, my sight improves," she says. Even though the lighting in the room hasn't changed, she experiences it as dark when she arrives and almost too bright when she opens her eyes after a powerful soul retrieval. In our experience, the surroundings become more vivid when more of the soul self is present in the body.

The more times Tia participated in the soul retrieval process, the longer she experienced a sense of calm, presence and well-being. This is common. When we first experience awakening through RTT, there may be a sharp contrast between the new awareness and the way we've been in the world. As we integrate the experience and begin to transform our lives more and more, feelings of empowerment, calm, and even euphoria are more commonplace. Staying present in the body then becomes more of an everyday experience.

Once our soul parts have expressed their truth, we fully anchor them in our bodies by validating them, replacing negative self- talk with loving words of thanks and affirmations from the heart. These words might be something like "Thank you for saving my life. You are the reason I kept going when I wanted to give up so many times. I realize now that I abandoned you. I only did what I was taught to do. I'm so sorry. I love you, and I thank you. Please forgive me."

The words expressed are intimately personal and individual. Each client is guided by his/her own inner voice, higher self, or wisdom during the soul retrieval process, and encouraged to find words that are personally meaningful. For those experiencing it for the first time, the facilitators are there to provide guidance and suggestions.

RTT helps us discover where the lost parts of our souls are residing, and we bring them home via participatory soul retrieval. We accept that in order for us to achieve our goal of inner peace and fulfillment, we must first join with the fullness of our soul essence. Soul recovery proceeds with greater ease when we have no agenda or expectation. When we set our intent to heal and surrender to the process, we unlock the key to our healing.

As with all aspects of RTT, I recommend that the initial phases of soul retrieval have a human witness—ideally, an experienced practitioner for many sessions. Each person will know when he/ she feels grounded enough in RTT work to complete participatory soul retrieval alone.

The level of client participation, even with a practitioner present, separates participatory soul retrieval from the traditional shamanic method. The retrieval itself is done by the client, with the witness or facilitator's encouragement and support to journey deeper, regardless of the intense emotions that may arise.

Becoming Whole: Mitch's Story

As we heal, we begin to construct a new belief system that serves us in becoming whole and healthy people. We gather ourselves from the past and future into the present moment, and can once again feel the bliss of being and the power of creation.

Mitch's story illustrates the union of the core emotional healing and participatory soul retrieval processes that we have come to call RTT. Mitch is an Alaska Native man who had long ago moved to what Alaskans call the Lower 48 (the 48 contiguous states). On a friend's recommendation, he decided to travel back to Alaska for a workshop at White Raven Center. He had two sons and was attempting to teach his younger son how to read. In his efforts, he found himself becoming frustrated and angry at levels he described as extreme. "My anger isn't proportionate to the situation. I mean, he's four years old, and I go into fits of rage and slam the table down and scare him for no reason. I overreact." Luckily, Mitch recognized that there was something else happening below the surface.

Our workshops typically begin at 6:00 p.m. on a Friday evening and run all weekend. Since Mitch's flight arrived Friday morning, he had time to explore. Having been away from his native land for so long, he thought it might be interesting to take a drive down memory lane. Soon, he found himself not far from the White Raven Center, at a trailer park where he had lived as a child with his mother and siblings. "I've lived on a lot of roads in my life, but that one is the only one I'll never forget," he later told me with sadness in his eyes.

When he located the trailer where he had spent many hours alone as a young child, hungry and cold, he wasn't yet aware that he had already begun his healing journey—even before the workshop started.

After his side trip activated repressed memories and traumatic episodes from his childhood, Mitch checked in at White Raven for the weekend session. He shared with us his love for his children, and his deep concern that he was traumatizing them as a result of his own childhood experiences. He was terrified that his reactionary behavior was out of control. Shortly thereafter, he headed into his first experience of RTT.

Mitch lay down on the mat and began to breathe deeply as I, in the role of the facilitator, helped him learn to connect to core feelings in his body while allowing his mind to rest. After about twenty minutes, I noticed a shift in his energy. I witnessed his body shiver, shake, and tremble, and I sensed he was feeling terror. I asked him what he was experiencing.

Quietly, in a childlike voice, he said, "I'm in the trailer I grew up in. I'm in this dirty trailer, sitting on a moldy mattress in the middle of the floor, and the room reeks of alcohol. There's dirty dishes piled sky high. It's cold because the heat's not on. I'm not sure if we have electricity. I remember it was always cold. I remember being so cold all the time. And nobody is here, as usual."

Mitch switched in and out of allowing his child self to share truth, interjected with comments from his adult observer self. I refer to this as "dual consciousness."

"That was the part that was the hardest," he continued. "I was tired of being lonely. I had no idea where my siblings were, and I didn't know where Mom was, which was kind of the norm. I'm here in this cold, dark trailer, and nobody's taking care of me. There's no food to eat except for some moldy Wonder Bread, but that's about it. And, oh, I was mad at my mom! I loved her to death, but I knew she was a terrible mother."

As the facilitator, I encouraged Mitch to allow for the experience of his five-year-old self and assured his adult self that he could continue to observe the entire process. As Mitch allowed his five- year-old self to share more of his truth, he gradually expressed a full range of emotions from terror to a broken heart to anger.

"How does being left alone make you feel?" I asked him.

The pain stored in Mitch's body was thoroughly activated. He began to express the full depth of the loneliness and anger he had felt as a little boy. He expressed intense anger toward his mother and the father he had never known. He grieved heavily there on the mat, experiencing what the little boy had been forced to repress in order to survive the insanity of his childhood. In turn, the adult Mitch became more conscious as he recognized patterns of behavior that had manifested throughout his life as a result of his childhood experiences. He began to see that it was the repressed child in him who was terrorizing his own children. "Yes, it did happen," I told Mitch, serving as witness to his experience. "This all happened to you."

At the time of the trauma, there in that trailer, Mitch's five-year old soul part escaped his body, automatically suppressing the pain in order to survive. During his RTT session, Mitch continued to move the pain that he felt in his core out of his body, experiencing both rage and grief as he cathartically sobbed and screamed. He was hurting and healing at the same time as truth rushed home to him. He then experienced what he described as a "skip" in time, moving quickly to another significant scene from his past. (This kind of "skip" to another space and time is not uncommon during the emotional processing of RTT.)

"This is really crazy. I'm in a different house or trailer, again on the same street and sitting in a bedroom," Mitch described. "I know I'm five or six years old, and I'm sitting on a mattress on a bed with cold steel frames. The mattress has piss stains on it and no sheets to cover them up. The room's a mess, but there isn't much in here anyway. I'm feeling lonely. I'm aware that my adult self is looking at my younger self, and instead of pain, I just feel numb."

I continued to prompt Mitch to fully feel the truth of what he was experiencing. This is when the pain began to intensify again, coming on in another wave as Mitch allowed his adult self to fully merge with his five-year-old self, finally expressing years of repressed anguish, grief and pain.

Mitch sobbed as he felt himself wrap his arms around his little boy self and begin to speak truth to the boy. As Tia had done, Mitch spent time loving his younger self and showering him with nurturing, kind, and gentle words. "All you wanted was a dad or mom and to know that you're not alone. I'm here now, and I want to comfort you. I love you, and I will never leave you alone," he said. Mitch saw himself in his mind's eye as an adult accompanied by his inner five-year-old. "I finally took his hand," Mitch described to me, "and we got up and went for a walk. I just knew that he needed to get outside because that trailer was the worst place in the world to be. And here I am giving this boy love and comfort, and it's actually happening. I'm healing this little boy, and I was able to tell him that it's not always going to be this way. And through that experience, I could tell that I was bringing that part of myself home. I felt like I could accept that my childhood was a part of me—that it happened."

Mitch then described experiencing what felt like parts of him still floating above his body. I encouraged him to invite those parts back home as well. When he did so, he felt a full integration happen, as a sudden rush of energy entered his body. Afterward, he said he felt a sense of calm and peace and as if he were more whole. Fragmented parts of Mitch's soul had come home.

After Mitch went back to his family, he was no longer triggered with fits of rage and frustration when he taught his sons. Parents who experience trauma at a certain age frequently become triggered when their children reach that same age. As a result of his soul retrieval, Mitch now connects to his boys as an adult rather than as a wounded child.

Opening to the Process

Every participatory soul retrieval process is a unique experience. Even clients who have experienced it many times will find that no two soul retrievals are exactly the same. They might take a journey into infancy, childhood, or even back to the womb. At other times they may see themselves as an adolescent, a teenager, or even a young adult. The soul part can be any age. They might even discover themselves in a setting of some ancient time, even though all of the people around them feel and look familiar.

My husband shared with me that during one of his first RTT experiences, he found himself crying hard as he rowed by a village of death in a canoe. "I felt incredible grief, knowing that my family and tribe had died from influenza or some other horrible disease. I could feel my hands on the paddle. I could see the village totem poles and the structures of the long houses. I could see that the vegetation growth had consumed the village. I felt that I was there at that moment even though

Participatory Soul Retrieval

I have never visited that village or paddled a canoe in my life. I don't have any idea where this place exists. I knew this body I was looking at was me. This body was my soul part that needed to be reintegrated."

Soul fragments may be associated with any phase of the current life cycle or even with past lives. The soul fragments that come home to us are generally connected to the core emotional traumas we are processing in the moment, whenever and wherever those traumas originated. Floyd felt incredible joy from reconnecting to his soul part from another lifetime.

When Floyd first began his processing, he was aware of a wolf. He could see the wolf standing maybe fifty feet away. Floyd was already aware of him most of the time and knew what the animal represented: "The wolf was my rage, my hate that I was not willing to express. I was afraid of what I might do, so I pretended it wasn't there. One day, I was ready, and I welcomed the wolf back into my body to help me express my truth and clear the energy."

"Later the wolf returned to teach me another lesson, and I ignored him again for many years," Floyd says. One day, he saw the wolf on the roof of our home. "He was standing there watching," Floyd explains, "and every once in a while, I would see him still there." Eventually, the realization came to Floyd that the soul part represented by the wolf was trying to teach him that home is not a place as he had grown up to believe. "Then, I saw this wolf turn and look at me like, 'Duh! You stupid idiot. I've been waiting for you to let me come back home,'" Floyd says. "And I breathed him back into me, and I said, 'I get it. Home is my body.'"

Participatory soul retrieval is a profound heart-opening experience—one that truly fills us up from the inside. We experience a sense of expansion as our soul parts integrate. Some have described it as feeling like giving birth to themselves. Clients often share that they feel like their power is back, their voice has returned, they feel present, and they are involved with life again. After integration occurs, many clients describe feelings of hope, trust, innocence, playfulness, joy and curiosity.

As a facilitator, I have observed changes in skin tone, more relaxed faces, bright eyes that were previously dull, and calmer body language. Clients who come to their session breathing shallowly are visibly breathing more fully afterward. They feel less tense and anxious. They feel lighter and frequently say that the outer world looks more vivid, bright, and colorful. They shift away from focusing on negativity and move toward a more positive outlook. The biggest transformation that the majority of participants describe, however, is a sense of inner calm and peace—something they may never have experienced before in their lives.

The process of soul retrieval, either participatory or traditional, has a huge impact on our ability to break soul-damaging contracts and beliefs. In chapter 10 we will talk about maintaining the peace we experience from RTT and soul retrieval, sustaining the presence of the soul parts in the body, and learning to nurture our souls in loving ways so that soul loss doesn't recur.

Soul retrieval defies description. It is giving birth to ourselves. It is welcoming ourselves home and reintegrating qualities we were born with—the hope, trust, innocence, playfulness or curiosity that may have been "lost" at the time we were wounded. It's truly one of the most beautiful and powerful experiences that human beings can have—fully opening our hearts to ourselves.

The Immediate Aftermath of Participatory Soul Retrieval

Sometimes, keeping soul parts separate from us is a way to avoid feeling certain emotions. If that's the case, bringing the soul part home will open the door to those emotions. If you have habitually denied your shame, for instance, you may actually feel more shame at first after soul retrieval. This can be disconcerting and difficult, and it can cause you to feel like maybe you've done the process wrong or that RTT is making you feel worse rather than better. You might attempt to control the soul part by repressing the emotions; after all, numbing those feelings was your well-learned coping mechanism.

If unpleasant feelings do arise after soul retrieval, RTT is the perfect process for continuing to move that emotional energy without judgment. It has come to the surface to be healed. So, as it rises, you have an opportunity to release pain that you have held on to for years. When that pent-up emotional energy does finally move through, you will feel a beautiful sense of relief. Just bear in mind that you might need to be patient as you wait for that experience.

"If we can share our story with someone who responds with empathy and understanding, shame can't survive."

—Brené Brown

"Trauma is a fact of life.
It does not, however,
have to be a life sentence.
Not only can trauma
be healed,
but with appropriate guidance
and support,
it can be transformative."

—Peter A. Levine

Chapter 5

RTT for PTSD, Emotional Trauma, and Abuse

Kent was deployed to Afghanistan in 2003 and Iraq in 2005. In 2006, he was formally diagnosed with PTSD. "At first, I thought I wasn't affected," he says. "But as time grew on, and the stress of living on my own got to me, I realized that I couldn't function independently well enough to take care of myself."

When he moved back home with his parents things improved, but not enough. "I had regular mood swings, unreasonable anger outbursts, and uncontrollable rage," he says. "I couldn't leave the house unarmed. I didn't feel safe anywhere. I felt as if I might encounter an intruder at any point."

Kent went back to school and had a very difficult time engaging with his fellow students. He felt completely isolated and cut off from everyone.

In 2009, through his sister, Kent learned of a female veteran who had worked with us at White Raven Center, and he could see how RTT had changed her. When he visited our website and read about what we do, he says that it didn't mean anything to him at first because he had no context for it. However, the differences in his sister's friend convinced him to sign up for the next available workshop in Alaska. He spent an intensive two weeks with us doing both private sessions and a workshop.

Rapid Transformation Therapy

Kent likens his first RTT session to the first time he ever jumped out of an airplane. "I was scared because I'm scared of heights, and at the same time, I didn't really know what to expect," he says. During his sessions, Kent went back to traumatic experiences during his time in the military. One of those experiences involved the death of eight people in his company. "I was able to grieve in a way that I never got to do while on active duty, and I never could bring myself to do while alone," he says. Through releasing the trauma of that event, he adds, "I don't have to feel guilty that I lived or I escaped unharmed."

"One of the biggest things that I dealt with, especially during that first workshop, is a lot of pent-up rage," he says. In his sessions, he yelled, screamed, and attacked a structure of plastic mats held firmly by a dozen participants as he kicked and punched. "I came at it like I was Godzilla going through downtown Tokyo," he says with a chuckle. Kent reports that after participating in a session, he usually feels exhausted. Feeling better comes a bit later.

Of his first workshop, Kent says, "There are no words to describe my experiences with others and with myself. I was able to sort out my truth and to see and take hold of who I really am underneath all of the emotional scarring."

"Before my work at White Raven," Kent continues," I was cautious, unsure of myself, afraid and alone, and most importantly, isolated. The only people who were really close to me were my immediate family and my dog, Max. If I could take a picture that would show all the pieces of my personality that have come out of hiding since starting my healing process at White Raven, anyone looking at it would think they were looking at two completely different people. Today I never feel isolated, no matter where I go in my life. I have many people now that I look forward to seeing on a daily basis. I have confidence in myself back, and the knowledge that I am a good person, capable of being loving and kind at the same time as being able to do the job required of an infantryman."

Kent says he isn't a new person; he has just become his true self. "I had insight and perceptive abilities before, but they got buried under trauma until all I could see was my own emotional state, and then only enough to know that something wasn't right. The work I've done at the White Raven Center and on my own has helped me clear that emotional detritus away, so that I can use those abilities once again."

When asked what his life would be like if he hadn't found RTT, Kent says, "I might not even be alive. I had considered suicide a couple times in the early days following my 2005 deployment. If I was still alive, I'd still be living with my parents right now most likely and I'd probably be on my way to alcohol abuse of some sort, whether it's just drinking an outrageous amount every night or just binge-drinking on the weekends or something. My life would be a lot emptier in a lot of ways, and I wouldn't have been able to get close to anybody. Now I have a steady job, and I've learned a trade. I'm a welder, and I don't have an alcohol problem or any other substance abuse problem. I'm in good physical condition, and my life is pretty good. I'm generally a pretty happy person. Five years ago, I was pretty miserable."

Kent is also now in a loving relationship with a beautiful woman, and he discovered a desire to learn how to dance and was able to let go of his worry that people would make fun of him because of it. He enjoys the new activity immensely.

He worries about his fellow veterans who fail to seek treatment for PTSD. "I think veterans often don't receive treatment for PTSD because they feel that nobody else can understand what they're going through. So why should they bother opening up to anybody? Before coming to White Raven I would lock the doors and double-check them, and I would walk around my home with a loaded pistol because I just didn't feel safe. Another vet at the workshop said, 'Yeah, I did the same thing. I double-checked and triple-checked my doors, and I made sure all of my weapons were loaded.' That's the kind of interaction, I think, that breaks down that sense of isolation. After my first workshop, it was no longer so important for me that people understand my experiences, and how my trauma affected me. I didn't have a need to make people understand anymore."

Kent also points out that he wouldn't want his loved ones to really "get it" because in order to do that, they would have had to experience the same traumas. "Why would you want them to have those experiences?" he says.

The Trauma of Childhood Oppression

While not all of us have experienced the trauma of fighting in a war zone, we have fought our own battles in our childhood homes—our own kind of war zone. This is why so many of us suffer from PTSD not so very much unlike that of our soldiers.

As you will see from the stories that follow, a primary cause of soul loss in children is the deprivation of their basic needs: love, nurturing, understanding, warm touch, freedom of expression, eye contact, compassion from adult caretakers, and the security that comes with the regularity of balanced meals. Children may be further oppressed by senseless acts of uncaring adults or by witnessing or directly experiencing acts of violence or inappropriate sexual activity. Another circumstance that can be oppressive to children is the sense from one parent or the other that they do not belong biologically to that parent. This sense may be so intense that the child spends his or her entire life trying to fit in or belong somewhere.

Severe childhood oppression can even lead to death. For example, we know of a twelve-year-old girl from my husband's village who was so depressed that she hung herself, and she is only one of many. Whatever form it comes in, childhood oppression contributes to soul loss because it causes the child to give up, accept that this is just how life is, and embrace the belief that "I don't really matter in this world." Soul loss from childhood oppression occurs because the pain of the experience is so intense, parts of the soul detach as a survival mechanism.

When children lose parts of their souls, they experience a tremendous sense of yearning, both for their own souls (this yearning is not conscious), and for love. They are constantly looking for someone to love them, becoming obsessed in their search and craving. Usually, they are looking for the parents' love. When they don't receive it, their search extends beyond the family as they reach puberty and adolescence. Older children, adolescents, teens and even adults search outwardly to be filled up by others. This can and does create unhealthy and even dangerous relationships which, unfortunately, just lead to still more soul loss.

Such unhealthy relationship patterns can also be traced through the introvert and reactive child personality types described in chapter 3. Extreme introverts, for example, do not trust other human beings, so they perpetuate a pattern of victimization in their lives. They get trapped in cycles of drama and either end up in relationships with reactive types who are stuck in the pattern of abusing introverts, or they connect with a person whose heart is closed. They find themselves pounding on the door of their partner's heart and become obsessed with manipulating someone into loving them. This person may end up giving away all of his/ her time, money, energy and resources—caretaking and begging to be loved— only to discover that it is never enough.

Reactive adults, for their part, most likely choose partners they can easily manipulate or control. Another relationship pattern is that of two highly reactive adults getting together and mirroring each other perfectly. These relationships can become highly explosive and spin out of control.

Rapid Transformation Therapy

All of these scenarios are examples of how we, as adults with untreated soul loss, perpetuate the triangle of victimization, perpetration, and caretaking. We reenact this triangle over and over again, in our personal lives and in the workplace.

If the family dynamics are compounded by the heavy use of alcohol or other drugs or by illegal activity, the child's experience becomes even more confusing and intense. For example, one client we had was trained as a small child to climb into grocery store dumpsters to look for edible food. Some of our adult clients were required, during their childhood, to clean up the house after every drunken party.

Scenarios like the ones you are about to read—scenes from the lives of Floyd, Toby, Bee, Arlene, Rebecca, Jan, Sherry, and Tia— leave children emotionally disconnected and in a mindset of pure survival similar to a war zone. They're always wondering, "When is the next bomb going to go off, and who is going to get hurt?"

The intent in sharing these stories is to give you, the reader, a deeper understanding of the RTT healing process. Each person's story reveals individual traumatic life experiences. Yet, once they progress to a place of knowing their own sense of peace and calm, once they can honestly say, "This did happen to me, and it is not happening now," they are no longer affected by their past traumas and are able to enjoy being present in life. As I always tell my clients, "We allow ourselves to move emotional energy in a therapeutic environment so that we regain the personal power to take action by choice. We are no longer emotional reactors as a result of our past."

Floyd's Story

"You must realize that what I am about to share did happen to me. I had no choice but to live the way the people surrounding me lived.

Yes, I did suffer; and yes, I did have good times despite it all. I am bonded to all of those I grew up with. I loved each and every one of them, and I still do. I miss them every day. When I reflect back, I feel gratitude and realize I have found what I have been looking for my whole life—peace with my past and the awareness that there is nothing to forgive. I can finally say I am truly living in the now."
—Floyd Guthrie

My husband, Floyd, exhibited the symptoms of acute PTSD resulting from a number of experiences in his life—sexual abuse, poverty, neglect, oppression and prejudice, war and alcoholism. When he was told that there was no cure for PTSD, he was discouraged to the point of giving up. As I previously shared, that's when we discovered the powerful core emotional healing process and began to develop the methodology of Rapid Transformation Therapy, which we continue to refine and practice today.

After years of doing RTT, Floyd's life has changed dramatically; the world in which he lives is now the polar opposite of the world where he grew up. "I had so much dark energy to clear to find home, but I am home now in my body. And my heart is open to this thing called life," he says.

Certainly, as a child, that was not the case for Floyd. "I had a lot of rage toward my parents because they didn't protect us," he says. "They couldn't pay for the garbage man to pick up the garbage, so as little kids, we had to take the garbage—paper bags, I think— and walk it down the hill to the dock and toss it off into the ocean every once in a while."

When Floyd was seven years old his father got a new job, and they moved from their small village to a city of 12,000 people. It was a "redneck" community with only about 2,000 Native people. Floyd had to enter grade school in his hand-me-down clothes that didn't fit properly.

"I walked right into that oppression," he says. "I was in the third grade, and they put all us Native kids in a group of our own. We were considered the stupid ones. The non-Native kids on the playground shamed us for being in the 'dunce class.' We were isolated and always treated differently."

As previously noted, the Native children had always been taught to listen rather than speak up and ask questions. Paying attention—listening to the voices and sounds around you—was important in their culture. Because the Native children were so quiet, they were considered dumb even though they knew the answers as well as the other kids.

Floyd remembers one instance where his teacher repeatedly scrubbed his hands because he was "dirty." "I realized she was trying to scrub my knuckles really clean," he recalls. "And I looked at her and said, 'Mrs. Butterfield, I think it's in the skin.' And her face turned pale. I just remember that look she gave me like chalk, and she turned and walked out of the room. I stood there for a moment and absorbed the shame that she put in me because my darker skin was 'dirty.' She planted it in me, that shame, and I believed her." This is an example of what Don Miguel Ruiz, author of several noted books including *The Four Agreements,* refers to as accepting the agreement of another as part of our belief system.

During his adolescent years, Floyd had to be very careful of the police. "They would kick the drunken Alaska Natives and beat them to death and just leave them there in the alley because the police could do that at the time," he says.

Floyd vividly remembers an incident as a teenager when he thought, "I wish I was white because things would be so much different for me." He possessed anger and shame that was overwhelming, and he turned most of it inward. One day at the age of fourteen, the anger broke out of him in a violent reaction to being teased. "This guy was bigger than me—six feet tall—and I was five feet, five inches tall and only 120 pounds. I wasn't a big kid at all," Floyd explains. "He started picking on me and laughing and laughing. He triggered that point in me, and the rage came. I found myself on top of him, and my fingers went into his eyeballs. I had three guys pull me off of him, and I just started to cry because I knew I could have blinded him. I had so much hate in me. And I was loaded with shame around being Native."

When Floyd took his first drink at the age of fifteen, he was immediately addicted. He points out, however, that he was mostly addicted to being numb. He couldn't bear to feel his feelings. "I felt numb all the time. I was not able to be really open with anybody. I just couldn't," he says. "When children aren't allowed to speak their truth, they bottle it up, and that becomes their truth. When you repress, you don't heal, and the numbed feeling is extremely addictive. People think they're at peace, but there's a tension there. No one can really touch you."

In 1968, Floyd joined the Army and was sent to Vietnam. This was after the battles had diminished but, for eleven months, he experienced the trauma of being in a combat zone.

With one month remaining to complete Floyd's tour in Vietnam and six months left in his term of active duty service, the Red Cross notified the commanding officer that Floyd's mother's liver had started to fail. Floyd was offered an option that would allow him to be discharged six months early if he would just stay for thirty more days before visiting his mother.

"I wanted to get out so bad," says Floyd. "But I felt I needed to go home and see my mom." Waiting for thirty days felt like too long, so Floyd turned down the offer of an early discharge, went to see his mother, then returned to serve the remaining six months of his tour of active duty in Fort Bliss, Texas.

When Floyd saw his mother she was tremendously bloated, and not long after his visit she died—essentially from her alcoholism. Soon after that Floyd's uncle disappeared; they found his body a month later. He had apparently fallen off the dock while drunk. Floyd's father passed away four years later by drowning in his own vomit—yet another person in the family to succumb to alcoholism. In 1992, when Floyd first experienced emotional release work with a team of practitioners

Rapid Transformation Therapy

from a well-established treatment center, he pounded a cushion until his knuckles were bloody. "This is how it feels inside of me," he thought at the time. Reflecting back, Floyd now realizes that when he walked out of that facility, he was still in process because the team had no understanding of how to bring closure to his experience.

Upon returning home to his village after that session, Floyd's whole body began to shake. This trembling continued for three weeks until the energy finally moved through him, helping Floyd shift into a calm state. "But my heart was still closed," he says. "The thing is that I was programmed to keep my heart closed, as I was taught to not feel. I had no reason to open my heart."

Floyd and our team at the White Raven Center recognize the importance of helping participants close each session safely. We prepare and educate each client about the steps that must be taken to comply with our strict safety guidelines, which include bringing the session to full closure, reframing the experience, assessing the need for follow-up support services, and teaching multiple tools for maintaining the energetic shifts achieved during the session. People come to us hurting, and the last thing we want to do is contribute to their pain—so we are conscious of never leaving clients alone, open and vulnerable, as they would be without that closure.

When I began working with Floyd, there was so much rage, pain, and shame that came out of him. He felt guilt about being a Vietnam veteran. He felt rage over the senseless loss of his parents and his inability to change the situation. He felt a lingering, unconscious shame, the effect of having been a child oppressed by the larger society. There were many repressed parts of Floyd that hated everything and everyone.

When a nearby village held a small ceremony to honor veterans there were only eight in attendance, so they were each asked to speak. When it came time for Floyd's turn, he said, "I don't deserve to be here. I wish I'd died over there."

His own words surprised him. After the ceremony, a woman came up to Floyd with an open heart and said: "You deserve to be here. My brother didn't come back. You belong here."

While the woman's words touched him, Floyd still couldn't forgive himself for not serving the way he felt he "should" have— in battles like so many others. In an early processing session, Floyd experienced a powerful soul retrieval in relation to his time in Vietnam. He saw himself in his mind's eye on a black field with trees, and there were soldiers inside the trees who hadn't made it back home. "I saw thousands of trees, and I walked among them," Floyd explains. "I was crying, and they said, 'You have to go home. You belong there. You deserve to live. This was my journey, not yours.' I broke down and cried, and I felt like I could actually see this part of me lifting out of Vietnam and shooting right back into my body. I felt incredible peace and forgiveness. Now I was able to say, 'I did my best, and I did serve my country. I deserve to be honored.' Not looking for it outside of myself anymore. I honor myself. I respect myself. I didn't care if the government cared."

Before that experience, Floyd had been unable to go to the Vietnam Memorial in Washington, DC. After the session, he was able to go there and feel pride, connection, and peace.

Today, as a result of the emotional clearing and soul retrievals that Floyd has experienced, he is a content man. "My heart is truly open to me after being closed for most of my life," he says. "I'm at peace with all that happened to me and to my people. I feel love, peace, joy and happiness. There is nothing to forgive anymore—nothing at all. In my mind, I can go back and visit the drunkenness and smell it as if it is happening now. I can see the violence. It's all there, and it doesn't affect me. It's like an art gallery. If we don't process through our pain, every picture from the past discharges all these feelings within us. I can look at the pictures now and even touch them, and they don't trigger me. And I recognize that all the ugliness made me who I am."

Toby's Story

I remember the day, a little over ten years ago, when Toby first came to White Raven Center seeking help. Floyd, myself, and another facilitator greeted him at the door. He was incredibly thin, had shaved his head, and looked meek and lifeless. We all thought he was dying.

Toby had struggled with severe, at times suicidal, depression for twenty years. For ten of those years, he drank alcoholically. In his early to mid twenties he was diagnosed with major depression, severe PTSD, borderline personality disorder, social phobia, panic disorder, dissociative disorder and obsessive-compulsive tendencies. In his twenties and thirties, the anxiety and panic were so debilitating that he was unable to function continuously at the high level he was capable of, and sabotaged jobs and many other opportunities.

As an example, when Toby was twenty-five, he received his Reiki attunements. The man who passed the attunements was impressed by Toby's level of sensitivity to the subtle movements of energy and invited Toby to apprentice with him in shamanic training. Toby thought about it for a few days and then replied, "I don't know what you think you see in me, but you're wrong." The list of opportunities sabotaged by Toby feeling unworthy and inadequate is long.

Toby shares, "Ever since I was a small child, I believed that I was unimportant, unworthy of love, undeserving of happiness, and generally inadequate. I can remember being so sensitive, feeling the people around me . . . when I saw someone in pain, it was as if their pain was mine. It scared and confused me. I learned how to present an image of myself that betrayed how I actually felt. I became a master of this. I learned how to close my heart to protect myself." Toby shared with me many times that there was no place for him in this world and that the only way to get someone to love and accept him would be through what he eventually learned were caretaking and co-dependent strategies.

Right before he came to White Raven Center, Toby had lost twenty pounds in a matter of three weeks. He wasn't sleeping, and he had lost the ability to keep solid food in his body. Four years before that, he had been in the hospital twice for a total of nine weeks. During that time he experienced a nervous breakdown, insomnia, straitjackets, padded rooms, self-inflicted injuries, twelve sessions of electro-convulsive shock therapy, a variety of medications, alienation from friends and family, and financial collapse.

Eight years before that, Toby was in a car accident while driving intoxicated. His neck was broken and his best friend, also in the car, died. In the year following that accident he was hospitalized for a total of six weeks with diverse challenges triggered by intense grief and guilt. The guilt fueled self-hatred and prompted repeated attempts to atone for "killing his best friend." What then lurked just beneath the surface of the desire to be of service was, in truth, a co-dependent and guilt-driven strategy to "make amends" for his wrongs.

"I've seen therapists who have worked with Vietnam vets and was told that the PTSD they saw in me was worse than most of the vets they work with," he says.

Toby had tried to take his own life on several occasions, and was experiencing suicidal feelings when he arrived for his first RTT workshop. When some people begin the RTT process, it's difficult at first to surrender to their emotions. Not so for Toby. "I knew that there were lessons that life was imploring me to learn. The time for subtle suggestions was over. Simply intellectually recognizing this pattern and being able to write a logical story in my mind that connected the dots between the past and present wasn't enough anymore, and I knew it. This pain had cracked me open so wide that it exposed and touched every open wound of longing and loss in my life," he explains.

His emotions were on the surface before he ever lay down on the mat and started breathing. "As soon as I opened my mouth and started talking, I was in process," he recalls. "And I think my first session was probably three and a half hours. One of the blessings of having so much emotion activated within you is that you just *go*. I sort of became the processing poster child. There was nothing that was going to stop me, and there was no self-consciousness. I was at the end. I was going to kill myself. I had nothing to lose. I fully surrendered."

Those first six months, Toby went to all of the workshops at White Raven Center and had two to three individual sessions per week as well. We often had him process first in a workshop because his ability to connect with his core emotions so fully triggered others in the room, helping them go deeper into their own process. "Inevitably, I would hit some rage and do a really big explosive session that would open everybody up," Toby says.

The sessions at White Raven Center were life-changing for Toby in a number of ways. "Never once did I feel anything less than completely accepted and loved," he says. "At the end of my first session I was exhausted, unable to move for half an hour. I lay in Marianne's lap with Floyd and others close by. As I lay there, my head being stroked by a woman I had only met three hours before, having exposed some of the darkest, most painful, shameful and self-loathsome parts of myself, I felt more sincerely cared for and seen than I could remember. These people had no judgment of me. They respected, honored, and accepted my experience as my truth. They knew—and practiced impeccably—that change can only come by first completely acknowledging and accepting what is. Each of them carried into their work with me an authenticity and integrity, for each of them had been on their own journey of healing and self-discovery and were not asking of me anything that they hadn't experienced for themselves."

"This was in sharp contrast," he explains further, "to my experience with countless 'healers' of the psychiatric profession who seemed more interested in insurance coverage, naming my 'illness,' and pathologizing my experience than in creating an atmosphere of love and acceptance where I could, without fear of judgment, explore my truth."

In fact, during his last hospital stay at the University of Pennsylvania's psychiatric ward, Toby was informed that he would need to take psychiatric medication for the rest of his life in order to properly function in society. Those professionals telling Toby that he would need to take medication for the rest of his life catalyzed his resolve to never again use pills to address his mental, emotional, and spiritual well-being. He shares being grateful to them and accepts that time of his life as a necessary step along the way to discovering a truth that resonates at the deepest levels of his being.

Toby acknowledges that taking this natural path has not been without its challenges. He has had relapses of depression that have called him to deeply question what healing ourselves truly looks like. "What I see is that even though some symptoms have persisted and have been activated at times throughout the last eleven years, my relationship with the experience of those symptoms has transformed. I no longer feel oppressed by my own experience. I see the truth in the awareness that suffering is not caused by what we resist, but by the resistance itself. The journey itself is our salvation. Presence with myself in the moment is the liberation."

Toby continues by sharing, "There is certainly no magic pill or shortcut, yet I can confidently say, after thirty years of investigating, exploring, surrendering to and practicing many different healing modalities and healing practices, that the RTT process is an invaluable, and in my case, vitally necessary part of the process of coming into a compassionate, powerful and loving acceptance of myself right now, exactly as I am. There is no more an 'enemy within.' I am no longer in opposition to myself. I have discovered that true wellness, true freedom, isn't actually about how you feel. It's about how you are able to meet and hold yourself, regardless of how you feel. It's about accepting yourself as you are in any given moment, rather than only accepting yourself when certain conditions are met. By that measure, I am very well."

We knew that by Toby following his feelings, by breathing into them and activating latent memories, doors would open and he would be guided to the source of his feelings.

"Ultimately," Toby says, "my friends at White Raven Center trusted and fully believed that I had the power to heal myself. They could guide, facilitate, encourage, love and support, but I had to be the one to choose to follow the threads of my feelings back to the source and reclaim the beauty, love, and light that is my true essence. I have discovered that it is truly one's own readiness to surrender to the simple truth of our immediate experience in the moment that allows for the shift to come into right relation with ourselves."

Where is Toby now? In the decade-plus since his first experience with RTT, Toby's life has completely turned around. From a suicidal place ten years ago, he is now a gifted facilitator and teacher for White Raven Center. He had already begun studying a wide variety of healing modalities around the world prior to coming to WRC, so he was able to move into a facilitator position fairly quickly. Toby continues his broad studies and is now one of the most knowledgeable people you will find on the subject of emotional and energetic healing.

"It's only because of doing so much of this work that I'm now available and present. I'm just very in my body. I'm *here*," Toby says. "I am no longer afraid of my feelings. I now see them as my teachers and my guides. To the extent I embrace my feelings, regardless of how painful they may be, I create within myself the love, safety, sense of purpose, self-honoring, and validation that I had, for so long in the past, sought outside myself."

Bee's Story

I vividly remember the telephone call I received approximately nine years ago from Bee, telling me that she wanted to kill herself. She was desperate for help and needed it *now*. Bee had called several psychologists' offices, trying to get in to see a therapist. The first available appointment was a month and a half out. Bee told the receptionist, "I don't want to kill myself in a month and a half. I want to kill myself now!" I met with Bee that evening and enrolled her in the weekend session that started the next day.

When Bee arrived for her first workshop, she shared with me that she had been on anxiety meds, depression meds and sleeping meds for sixteen years. Bee said her parents weren't loving. They were very strict and very abusive physically, mentally, and spiritually. "I was the product of rape of my mother by my father, and my mother didn't want me," she says.

"I was a tool to hurt my biological father. My mother was my worst tormentor. I was alone, facing the world mostly on my own, as young as two or three years of age. My mother humiliated me in front of people with verbal attacks and beatings. Suicide had been a part of my life for many years. I was living in a self- inflicted cell of self-hate and didn't even realize it. I used to have dreams a monster was chasing me, hurting me, and when I faced the monster, it always turned out to be my mother," Bee says. "My mom's motto was 'Do unto others before they do unto you. You never forget, you never forgive, you pay back.' Any sign of emotion, and she would go for the jugular. She would say things that would hurt, and there were a lot of beatings. It was just like a lash every time, and she'd keep going until she broke you down. And I learned how not to break down."

At the age of five, Bee prayed and begged God every night to kill her so that she could live in heaven with him. "That's a pretty young age to want to die!" she says incredulously.

As a child Bee had kidney problems, and her mother would shame her in public because the young Bee couldn't tell when she had to urinate. "We'd be in a store, and I'd just pee all over myself. She'd grab me up and start beating on me and yelling at me, and everybody was watching," Bee recounts.

Bee's mother never hugged or touched her in a healthy way. Like most children, Bee felt this treatment was her fault, and she tried with all her might to make her mother love her. Nothing ever worked. Because of her mother's distance, the two of them never really bonded.

"When she had cancer the last two years of her life," Bee says, "I had a hard time because I didn't feel grief or sorrow. And I had quite a few processes [at WRC] on that. And then, Marianne and Floyd helped me realize that my mother had never built a relationship with me, not a close one. So there wouldn't be sorrow or grief because there was no close-knit relationship. But that took a while to get over." Bee had to work through her own judgments that she "should" feel grief.

As is also frequently the case, Bee ended up marrying men who were much like her mother—two of them, in fact. "When I was eighteen, I got pregnant and miscarried, and my parents wouldn't stay around me. I had to dig the fetus out of the toilet myself, while Mom and Dad went to look at boats because they wanted to buy one. So I've pretty much always been on my own emotionally," she says.

When Bee arrived at White Raven Center, it was her last outreach for help. "I had lost my job, lost my home, and was a single parent with three kids. I had to move back in with my folks for them to help support my children and me, and I felt like a failure," she says.

"Oh God, I was so terrified to walk into the White Raven Center!" she recalls. "I was scared to death to have these people see me, let alone hear my story, and to possibly judge me for my sins. I told myself that I had nothing to lose and that I had endured a lot of things much harder than this. So I forced my feet to move forward one step at a time. I did not talk to very many people, I kept my eyes downcast, and I sat in a corner with all the cement walls I could muster standing in front of me. I was too deep in my own shit to acknowledge another person or be friendly.

The atmosphere was bright, warm, and the loving energy inside was overflowing and comforting. The people who had already been doing their work were bright, bubbly, cheerful, living in life. The room seemed to glow brightly from the colorful and bright auras emanating from these people. This place felt like a dream I was witnessing from the other side of the window. My ego mind kept telling me that this place was the twilight zone, and these beautiful people would turn into monsters any second. So I was distrustful of the feelings of love and acceptance I felt from these people who were welcoming me. At first I thought their happiness was fake, but as I watched them interact with different people at the workshop and actually got to know them, I realized that whatever they had, I wanted it."

During her first processing session, Bee began the breathing and soon connected with her emotions. "I started to cry, which eventually turned into wailing. I cried for all the injustices done to me, I cried for my lost childhood, I cried for my children, I cried for all the horrors I endured, and I cried for the mistakes I had made in my life. After a while, with Marianne and Floyd gently and lovingly guiding me, I was able to release a lot of the pain I had been poisoning my body with and brought back a soul part that been lost for many years. The feeling that came over me was nothing I had ever experienced before in my entire life. I felt a warm light of pure love wrap my whole body inside itself and nurture my soul. I started crying again, but this time from joy. I had felt the purest form of love that filled up my whole body and soul. I stayed in that place of pure love for quite a while."

After the workshop, Bee shared with us: "What I felt after each process was a floodgate of love. Everything looked brilliant and fresh. I left feeling like my life was worth living again. That was when I decided to get off all the uppers and downers my doctor had prescribed. I knew I had found something better than the drugs!"

Bee admits that her growth in the years since she began RTT hasn't always been easy, yet the benefits have been many. "With each part of myself that becomes healed, I have been able to let go of behaviors that have harmed me in the past, including self-judgment, self-hate and self-unworthiness," Bee says. "I have learned how to open my heart and to forgive. I have fought against centuries of cruelty passed down from generation to generation. I have fought with my worst enemy which was/is me . . . or what my ego calls 'me.'"

Bee is no longer suicidal, and she now celebrates her life. "I know when I'm triggered now, and I know when my heart is closing. I know when I space out that I have processing work to do. And I've also been able to be happy. The first forty-some years of my life were not happy. Now, most of the time, I feel happy. And I look at life with a positive mindset instead of always seeing the negatives in everything. I've been to psychologists, I've been to counselors, I've been to religious counselors, and nothing works like RTT."

Bee feels that talk therapy kept her in her head, analyzing over and over without any change. She believes RTT allows her to get out of that analytical habit, which has been a "tremendous relief."

Finally, Bee says, "This place really saved me. It's not easy work, but I know I'm getting better. I love this place. This is a safe place. Outside, I have to keep it under control and in a package, but this is where I can really be me. I know whichever mood I'm in, nobody judges me for it except me."

Arlene's Story

Arlene is a social worker who discovered our work through a coworker, then attended a group session that I conducted at a conference. As Arlene remembers it, "Marianne was doing some relaxation exercise, and as a part of it said, 'Okay, now I want you to think back to a time where you were hurt or somebody you cared about very much hurt you. Just keep breathing.' The energy that started to come out of my body was just so much sadness. I mean, tears were just streaming down my face, and I couldn't stop. Prior to that point, I would never let myself cry about things. I saw it as a sign of weakness."

It was the first time Arlene had ever allowed herself to feel those emotions, and she knew she needed to take a workshop at White Raven Center. Yet she put it off for another two years. Then, when she was eight months pregnant, she became "scared to death." Arlene came to us and said, "I'm going to be a mom. Help me." She didn't want her kids to feel responsible for her emotions.

Arlene shared with me that she was afraid when she arrived for her first workshop. "I knew this was good, but I was scared. I didn't know these people. I don't trust people. What a wacky concept of going to stay somewhere overnight," she says. When it came her time to share at the beginning of the workshop, she immediately began to sob and yell. The emotions bubbled up, and she was in process. Arlene remembers hearing someone say "Get the bat." This means that repressed anger was activated within her, and it was clear that she needed to use the plastic bat and pad—one of our tools for safely releasing anger. (This is only one of many ways to safely release anger; I always ask participants to tune in to what the body says it needs to do.)

"I hadn't been exposed to anything like that prior," Arlene says. "I had never witnessed anybody really raging. I had no clue. The facilitators told me, 'Keep your eyes closed.' I said, 'Okay,' and then I opened up my eyes and saw a red mat. Marianne had given me the bat and said, 'Go after it.'"

Arlene hit the mat so hard with the bat that she blistered her hands. Afterward, she felt a big shift. "That was the first time after having that rage session that I can tell you, I felt some sort of peace inside my body and inside my mind at the same time. So it was really a foreign experience, and it was so awesome," she shares. "I knew that I had to keep coming back. If I could feel that for that one moment in time, there has got to be the possibility for me to feel that longer and longer and longer. I just didn't know how to do it because I was so angry."

What was Arlene angry about? "My world was flipped upside down when my parents got divorced when I was a teenager. My mom had had a relationship outside of the marriage and had gotten pregnant. For a lot of reasons we didn't understand at the time, she left us with our dad, and he had started drinking pretty heavily," she says.

As a result, Arlene felt a lot of hatred toward her mother. The family didn't know how to function because her mother had been a stay-at-home mom. "It was easy to hate somebody who wasn't there," she says.

"I was afraid of really speaking the truth and saying what I wanted to say. I was also really scared of how strong I was. I knew I could probably kill somebody if I wanted to. Sports, thank God, saved my life. If I wasn't playing college volleyball and channeling that negative, really hateful energy into something . . . I try not to think about what my life would have been like if I didn't have that. So I stopped being as vocal.

I wasn't my authentic self, which wants to confront every injustice I see. I started swallowing all this [emotional] junk. Then, when I came and processed that, it felt so good to let that out and say the horrible things that I needed to say that were in my body. And then look around and see that, for real, [the other workshop participants] weren't judging me."

As is the case with many people, Arlene didn't know how angry she was. In retrospect, she has come to realize that she related to anger as her best friend, yet she wasn't aware of it at the time and didn't know it was unhealthy. "If you would have told me that I was angry, I probably would have laughed at you like, 'You're insane. I'm not angry.' I'm forty years old, and I've wasted so much of my life being mad."

The work has had a positive cumulative effect on Arlene's life. "My husband notices a huge difference when I come here. He notices I'm way more calm, I'm way more centered. I used to be so angry," she says.

Arlene points out that prior to doing this work, "I'd be driving down the street and just yelling at people, things like 'You're going too fast, too slow, you're in my way!' I don't get road rage anymore; that doesn't exist for me. In fact, when I see other people do it, I'm like, 'Wow, you could really use a session or two at WRC. Clearly, this isn't about driving. There is something else going on with you.'" Arlene shares that she now has unlimited compassion for other people. She sees people from a gentle place instead of the angry, judgmental place of the past.

Even now, Arlene acknowledges that she still gets nervous every time she walks into WRC for a workshop. "There is a part of me that wants to run away, and that's the part that needs to heal. As long as I feel that way, I know I need to keep coming," she says. "It's funny. When you come in, you're like 'Oh, shit, I'm not sure I want to be here.' Then, when it's time to leave, you're like, 'Oh, shit, I don't want to go back out there in the world.' It's so funny how fast that happens."

Reba's Story

Several years ago, Reba flew herself and her roommate to Anchorage and White Raven Center from Washington state for a week's stay. Reba was in a giant caretaking role with her friend, and although she wanted to heal herself, her focus was primarily on healing her friend. After experiencing the RTT process, Reba realized that she desperately needed help herself and decided to move to Anchorage on her own for that purpose.

Reba defines herself as a Christian who has found RTT to be harmonious with her faith. She came into the work trusting that it was for her good and praying, "God, I'm going to say yes to everything. I'm going to trust that you will protect me and that you will keep from my mind, my spirit, and my soul whatever things are not supposed to be there because at this point, I don't trust myself. I don't know when to say yes, when to say no. So that's your job. I'm going to leave that in your hands, and I'm going to say yes to everything."

Reba says her faith has been strengthened through the processing she has done at WRC. "I have the best relationship with God and with Jesus Christ that I've ever had in my life," she says. "I was raised in an evangelical church all my life, and this process has gotten rid of the garbage that was between me and Him. I've had many sessions where I would just cry and say, 'God, why don't you like me? I know you hate me. All I want you to do is love me. Just love me. And I know you don't like me the way I am.' In one process there was this black hole, and I thought, 'Okay, I'm going to go in this black hole and see what's going on.' It was like a round tunnel, and I couldn't see anything. I was feeling my way down this tunnel, feeling the walls, and then I came into this cavern that was really bright but not from the sunlight. The walls were effervescent. It was kind of wavy or bumpy on the walls, and I walked in, and way across the room, I saw someone. When he got closer, it was Jesus, and he walked up to me. He took my hand and said 'I love you.' And I just started bawling my eyes out. I couldn't even talk. Floyd was doing that session, and I couldn't even tell him what was going on. I was crying too hard. All I could say was, 'It's Jesus. It's Jesus!'"

Another time, Jesus's image came to her while she was processing and said, "I want to show you something." In her mind's eye, he took her hand and led her to the top of a hill that overlooked an indescribably beautiful valley. He then said, "See all of this? All of this and more is what I'm going to show you for your life. More beautiful than you could ever imagine."

Reba says that in her faith, she was taught that the imagination just makes things up and that God doesn't use the human imagination. But she has changed her belief about this. Now, she says, "Imagination is an amazing gift. It's a gift of storytelling."

She has even said yes to metaphorically killing her mother in more than one session, well aware that she was using her imagination for her own healing. Reba was abandoned by her mother after her little sister was born. It took Reba a while to have the courage during a processing session to let her small child self tell her mother exactly how she felt about the abandonment. Now she is no longer triggered by the memory of her mother, and she no longer feels the need to process issues about her mom. She isn't even triggered by people who behave like her mother, as had repeatedly been the case before RTT.

In one of her sessions, Reba was breathing in order to begin her RTT process, and she suddenly felt a sensation in her chest. "Someone is tapping, stabbing me in my chest!" she told the facilitators. "He's got a sword. He's stabbing me with a sword in the chest." Suddenly, in her mind's eye, she saw a sword next to her. She grabbed it and began to have a sword fight with this man in her vision. "It's a medieval knight, and he's trying to kill me!" Reba wasn't sure what was going on, but in the spirit of saying yes to everything, she went with what came up for her in the session, trusting that it was presenting itself to her for a reason.

At some point in the process, after Reba had seemed to move the emotional energy, the facilitator said to this knight, "It's 2014 now, and it's time for you to go." As soon as the facilitator said that, Reba says she saw a confused look on the knight's face, and he stopped fighting her. The facilitator then helped Reba release the knight and ask him to move on. "It was incredibly powerful and very vivid," she says.

The emotional benefits from an experience like this are enough. We don't seek to understand from an intellectual standpoint who the knight might have been, whether he ever actually existed, or why he was there. The point is that the experience brought her peace and healing, and that's all that matters.

Another benefit of RTT for Reba has been a new experience of her physical body. She says that she always thought she was in touch with her body—until she experienced RTT. In one of her first sessions, Floyd asked, "What do you feel in your physical body?" And she answered, "I don't feel anything. I feel nothing." It had become such a defense mechanism to not feel the deeper feelings that she simply disconnected from her body. She no longer has the need to disconnect.

One of Reba's key soul retrieval experiences happened as a result of having once given up a baby for adoption. She found herself raging at her younger self, absolutely furious that she would get pregnant and give up her baby. Then, after she had moved the angry energy, the facilitator said gently, "This was just a girl who didn't know what she was doing. Can you feel any compassion for her?"

Once Reba was able to contact her compassion for her younger self, she could invite that part of her soul back home. The experience was profound. "It felt like a tsunami of a rainbow, and it was like this rainbow was just washing over me—like a waterfall rainbow. It kept gushing and gushing and gushing over me for a couple of minutes. I felt ecstatic and just lay there for a while basking in it. I felt this tremendous sense of peace, joy, completeness and wholeness. I thought, 'I don't ever want to move again in my whole life. I'm just going to stay here because this feels really good.' It was an amazing feeling."

Today, Reba has begun the process of learning how to become an RTT facilitator. She is in training, and she didn't take on that role until she had done a lot of processing work herself. All of the facilitators at White Raven Center have worked for years on themselves, and those participants who have a calling can evolve into the role of facilitator over time.

"There was a lot of stuff that I needed to deal with at different ages," Reba says. "I had to go back at different ages, all the way back to infancy to deal with my mom." Now, she says, "I experience joy very often, which I never did before. When I realized I'd been joyful for like a week, I said, 'What's up? This is crazy!' Just smiling a lot and being really comfortable with myself. I'm very anxious to see what the future holds now, because there's more healing to come and more adventures to experience."

Sherry's Story

Like Floyd and Claire, Sherry had an experience in RTT that seemed to point to a past life trauma. As far back as she could remember, Sherry recalled disturbing dreams of loud trains going by her house. The sound of a train was so real that it would wake her, causing her to scream for her mother in the middle of the night. As an adolescent, the dreams intensified into vivid episodes of the train reaching the summit of a hill and exploding down the other side, heading straight for her bedroom.

In her young adult life, Sherry wondered why she repeatedly found herself living near railroad tracks and train stations. In her mid thirties, she came to White Raven Center. While deep in a process, she experienced an apparent past life memory in which she was a man who had committed suicide by throwing himself in front of a train. This man left behind a wife and five children and, after his death, his spirit was filled with grief and remorse over what he had done.

In allowing herself to remember and fully process this past life experience, Sherry was able to clearly see how many situations, relationships, patterns of behavior, and previously unexplainable triggers and events pointed to the past-life suicide.

Since experiencing the soul retrieval as part of this RTT session, Sherry is no longer triggered when she hears a train go by. In fact, Sherry has discovered that she no longer ends up living next door to train tracks anymore.

Jan's Story

When Jan first came to us, she was in a very unhealthy relationship. Little did she know at the time that her partner was a blessing in disguise, as he was activating the pain that lay dormant within her being. This pain was rooted in childhood trauma and coated in shame, and it wanted to be expressed.

Jan took a six-month break between the first workshop she attended and the next session, then processed for seven months straight after that, sometimes coming to WRC two to three times a week. She was absolutely committed to transforming her life. Her story is an example of the rapid transformation that can occur when a person fully commits to his/ her recovery and allows nothing to get in the way.

Jan says she "brought pieces of myself in buckets" to WRC the first time she came to us. "I was already broken up, and I was like, 'Here are all the broken pieces, and I don't know what to do with it. I'm just such a mess.' I felt like I was smashed. From a soul aspect, I really feel like I was incredibly fragmented. I always kind of wondered if I was verging on a split personality. I felt like there were deeply divided parts of me inside. It's not enough to say that I was distraught, and it's not enough to say that I was in tears. And I think that I had been for all my life. WRC was the first time and place that I could be really honest about it," she says.

Jan had scary dreams as a child that left her feeling like she was crazy. Her mother took Jan to a psychiatrist, who put Jan on antidepressants. "I harbored this feeling inside that I was crazy, and White Raven Center was the place where I started to realize that I was not, in fact, crazy."

Even after her first workshop experience, Jan noticed definite changes. It was the best she had ever felt, so she left thinking "I'm fixed!" Six months later, she realized that maybe she wasn't exactly "fixed" and still had some work to do, so she returned for another workshop. "It's a really interesting thing as an adult to look at yourself and realize that you have emotions, that it's probably normal, but that you literally have no clue how to deal with them," she says. "Then, to have enough intellect to say, 'Oh, I should really have those [tools]. Why don't I go get some?'"

Jan has a memory of a specific time when she was a little girl that she locked herself into her bedroom and cried in the dark, feeling sad and heartbroken. There, alone, she had an image of a woman who held her and rocked her like a mother would. During one of her RTT sessions, she re-experienced her little girl self locked in her bedroom, and the woman who rocked her was herself as an adult. "In a way," Jan says, "you could say that the transformation in my life has been becoming that person." She has been transformed into someone who is capable of mothering herself.

In twelve months' time, Jan experienced changes that she calls nothing short of amazing. She explains: "Just a year ago, I could have easily reeled off a list of all the things going wrong with my life every day, but now I have to stop and think back to remember what they were—feeling chased or pursued for no reason; being unable to even trust myself; an almost frantic need to check behind closed doors, under the bed, and behind the shower curtain; trying to fall asleep on the edge of an anxiety attack, unable to draw a full breath; outbursts of tears or anger triggered by the smallest things; meltdowns in the face of minor crises; a deep feeling of unworthiness for anything good that happened to come my way; and a great difficulty forming healthy close connections with others."

Today, Jan trusts herself and can better discern when others are worthy of her trust. "I can imagine myself living into old age," she says. "I can look others in the eye without being terrified of what they'll see in me. I no longer need to audit my behavior and speech. For the first time in my life, my self-image is of a beautiful adult woman, not a little girl or a scrubby teen. For the first time in my life, I am enough. Instead of looking for someone else to be my beloved, I can confidently say that I am the beloved, and I can mean it! Even better? I actually feel good about my life and about myself."

Jan is now in a vibrant, healthy relationship after a long history of what she deems as unhealthy ones. "It truly had never occurred to me beforehand that you could have a relationship without conflict," she says. "It's not like we're perfect. We have our fights every once in a while just like everybody else, but it's actually harmonious and nourishing. It's important to note that it's not that I've learned to act like I'm in a harmonious relationship. I'm not faking it in hopes of making it. I've actually found a harmonious relationship. Holy crap! Who knew they existed? And that's just another manifestation, because I am aware on a couple of levels that I would not be able to be the person that I am in this relationship if I had not done all this work on myself. We would have driven each other nuts by now."

Jan says she was even worried that life would be too boring without the drama. "But life is very much not boring. It's good," she says.

Jan is an example of what happens when we are emotionally (or physically) abandoned as children and end up, as adults, projecting that unresolved trauma onto others. In this situation, we unconsciously set ourselves up to be abandoned again and again. This is the universe's way of helping us wake up to the truth that we are abandoning *ourselves*. Every time we get in a relationship, if we have not dealt with our abandonment issues, we recreate the buried trauma and project the core belief that "those I love are going to leave or abandon me." If our partner does not leave, we may set the stage for the abandonment by rejecting them first, saying things like "You're going to leave anyway. Everyone I love always does."

These cycles damage our souls and, if untreated, contribute to the perpetuation of intergenerational trauma. When we don't have an understanding of this cycle, we become unconscious emotional reactors and fail to take action by choice. Each time we get triggered around these unhealthy patterns, it's an opportunity to heal. If we refuse to accept the opportunity and remain unconscious, we continue to repress our core emotions and prolong our own suffering. Fortunately, through processing with RTT, Jan was able to release the trauma of her early abandonment and stop the projection. This allowed her to finally attract a healthy relationship into her life.

Tia's Story

You have already read about parts of Tia's soul retrieval experiences. As I already mentioned, she was abused physically, mentally, emotionally and sexually by her biological mother's boyfriends, starting when she was a baby. The first time I worked with Tia in one of our rural Alaska communities, a local mental health practitioner had set up the session and accompanied me to observe. Shortly after Tia began the breathing process, she blacked out. During the time that Tia was "away," I met twelve other personalities in that first evening. Honestly, I did not know how to help Tia heal, and yet she kept coming back. So I engaged in a process of learning while supporting her through my presence. Tia's incredible healing journey is a result of her determination, perseverance, and unwavering commitment to change her life. She never gave up on herself, and I never wavered in my belief that she could heal.

Tia presented one of the most horrendous and graphic histories of childhood abuse I have ever heard. When she was only three years old, her mother commanded her to stop hiding beneath the bedcovers as her mother walked out of the room, leaving little Tia in the presence of a naked adult man. As she got older, she was abused further by other male acquaintances in her life. Her mother's boyfriend's son, who was eighteen years old, tied Tia and her sister up while playing "cowboys and Indians." He would then take each of them, one at a time, to a different room and sexually abuse them. Tia was eleven before she told anyone about the abuse she was experiencing. This led to all of the children being taken from their mother permanently, put into foster care, and eventually adopted.

As a result of her experiences, Tia developed dissociative identity disorder or DID (formerly called multiple personality disorder). In order to survive the insanity of her abuse, Tia developed and has experienced thirty-two distinct personalities.

I have processed with every one of them. Tia credits RTT with helping her to integrate most of these personalities. We continue our work together with the focus and intent to integrate all of them, as they are each allowed to express truth, heal, and evolve.

What is the experience of dissociating like? "It's like I just fade away or go to sleep," Tia explains. "It's kind of like in movies when people die and their spirit starts to float above them." The dissociations apparently began when she was very young. In school, her teachers would become angry because Tia would refer to herself as "we."

"It was about five years ago that I had a counselor finally able to pinpoint what was going on with me because I was having blackouts, and I was having what my kids called 'mood swings,'" Tia explains. She experienced lost time, and objects showed up that she didn't recognize. There were drawings that her husband told her she drew, yet she had no memory of having drawn them. People she didn't recognize would speak to her and tell her about the conversation they'd had with her days before.

Tia was skeptical about trying RTT at first. "They [the facilitators] just really listened. I felt comfortable. They never gave up, and they never made me feel like I was a monster or crazy or anything. There were many times I wanted to give up, but something inside me just kept me going," she says.

Interestingly, due to the DID, Tia wasn't fully aware that she was speaking out loud during her first RTT session. She was having a conversation with her soul part, but she didn't realize until others in the room responded that it wasn't an internal conversation and that she could be heard speaking.

As Tia experienced, it isn't uncommon for some people to go deep within while processing. It's much like a dream state when you're traveling and wake up unsure at first where you are. I had a similar experience the first time I processed. I had no idea where I was when I came out of it. I thought I was in a hospital because everything was white; I didn't remember right away that I was at a workshop. It took a while for me to adjust and recall where I was.

In the beginning, there were times when Tia dissociated during a session and wouldn't remember any of it. We started videotaping some of her sessions because she wanted to know what was happening. Tia's sessions could be enormously challenging at first because I learned that in order for her to heal, each personality had to engage in his/her own healing process. This would take hours and had to happen, as it would be irresponsible to leave Tia in a vulnerable state with a process not complete.

Certain emotions still trigger Tia to dissociate. However, after having experienced RTT for several years, she is better able to communicate consciously with her personalities and even prevent herself from dissociating. "There's a lot of times that I can feel when I'm starting to drift away, or I can feel a revolving door. Then there's times that I definitely have gotten a lot better where I can pull myself back or bring myself back," she says. She can sometimes shift the dissociative process before it takes place because she has developed greater awareness of her triggers, and how it feels when she begins to dissociate.

The intensity of Tia's triggers, including her anger, have diminished. In the past, her anger escalated to the point that she would do something like punch her car window until it shattered. Now she is much more likely to control that impulse. If she watched a TV show or film that depicted abuse, it could trigger her to dissociate. Now, she says, she might feel somewhat triggered but not usually to the point of dissociating. She is much more able to stay "home" in her body. If she finds herself becoming triggered she practices self-talk, reassuring herself that what happened to her was in the past. "It's no longer happening, and the abuse is taking place on television, not in real life," she tells herself. Remember that our child soul parts who are not yet retrieved or integrated live as if the trauma is still happening, so the self-talk is to calm those parts of the self that are still in need of healing.

Tia also has a history of self-harm behaviors such as cutting and burning herself. "I don't know how to explain it," she says, "but something would bother me, and I couldn't share it or express my feelings because I was always afraid I was going to hurt somebody. So it turned to self-punishment, I guess. All of a sudden I'd get angry, and I'd just feel like I'd have to burn or cut myself. Then there were times I'd go to sleep and wake up with burns." RTT has helped Tia to diminish the frequency of these behaviors. There is still work to do, yet she has made significant progress.

Tia's daughter has noticed that her mother is calmer and more relaxed. Tia is also speaking up for herself more in her life, and asking for what she needs. Additionally, she is better able to be there for others. "I can actually be there for somebody and not be triggered," she says, still somewhat surprised by her progress. "I can actually listen to them, and we can connect instead of my being disconnected and superficial."

The journey with her family has been a difficult one. "I've got a brother who went into the service, he says so that he could kill people because of his anger from his abuse. I've got a sister who's totally blocked it all out. I've got three other brothers who all went to prison for child abuse. The older one went and joined the circus. So my family is so screwed up. I'm the only one that's seeking help," she says. "This work here at WRC helped me to be able to say, 'Well, this is my story. It did happen and it is not happening now.'"

"I really think that if it wasn't for this place, and if it wasn't for Marianne and Floyd, I would be dead or prostituting. I got busted for that. I was headed down a real dark road," Tia admits. "I am very thankful for this place. I'm very thankful that I was able to come and participate and be a part of it. I'm not so angry anymore. I'm not a victim anymore. And my self-image isn't so low anymore. I don't feel like I'm worthless. I don't feel like I don't belong." Recently, Tia was awarded a service dog, Oscar, to be her companion. Since Oscar has been with Tia for the past month, she has not dissociated once.

"Recognition
of your addictions
requires inner work.
It requires that you
look clearly at the places
where you lose power
in your life,
where you are controlled
by external
circumstances."

—Gary Zukav

Chapter 6

RTT for Addictions and Their Aftermath

Addiction is clearly a symptom of a loss of connection with parts of our own souls. Addictions are a way to hide from ourselves when self-judgment, self-hatred, shame and guilt shape a self- image that we don't wish to face. While we most often think of addictions to substances, such as alcohol, caffeine, nicotine and heroin, we can also become addicted to work, relationships, food, exercise, sex, caring for others, or almost anything that removes us from being present with our own feelings.

Addictions reflect a loss of faith in ourselves and our capacity to create joy and fulfillment from within. RTT teaches us how to fill ourselves up with our own soul essence, which is the only thing that can ever truly fill us up. While RTT can have a profound impact on healing from addictions, ultimately the shift can only occur with the participant's willingness and intent to change self-destructive behaviors. The stories presented in this chapter illustrate how deeply addictions can be healed when we are courageous enough to fully surrender to the process.

Daniel's Story

Daniel grew up in a conservative and charismatic Christian home, in what he describes as an "intense spiritual environment." One of the byproducts of this environment was sexual suppression, with little value given to a solid education about sex and sexuality. When Daniel was twelve years old, his father died in a plane crash while working as an aid pilot overseas. The loss left a gaping void in Daniel's life.

This laid a foundation for an addiction to pornography that, helped along by the rise of the Internet, reached a peak when Daniel was married at the age of twenty-one. "There was this huge, whole erotic world that I had never been exposed to, never seen," Daniel recalls. He felt blindsided by his life, and the only place he knew to turn was the religious establishment that claimed to hold the keys to freedom.

"My wife and I started going to the biggest church in town, where the pastor had this book called *Every Man's Battle: Winning the War on Sexual Temptation*. It was really the first major book that came out in the Christian world dealing with pornography. I was desperate for this!"

Daniel was able to open up and be honest with some men he knew at church, and soon he found out that the book seemed to be speaking some truth. It seemed that every man he knew was dealing with the same issue. Daniel says that the book's directives were to "hate your sin and don't look at stuff." After reading it, he managed to stop looking at porn for about six months and then "crashed hard." His first thoughts? "I'm a failure. I'm *such* a failure."

This deep shame and guilt brought Daniel to the edge. He was ready to end it all when his brother-in-law, Nathan, decided to intervene. Nathan had been coming to White Raven for RTT. As a result, Daniel had seen some radical transformation in Nathan's life: "He went from a guy who just couldn't go a minute without smoking weed and living in our garage and dead-end jobs, to becoming a healthier guy. And he moved out, was living on his own, was starting to figure some things out, was able to hold down a good job. He was becoming somebody that I was respecting," Daniel shares. Having witnessed those changes helped Daniel listen to what Nathan had to say.

Although Daniel had been taught that indigenous spirituality was "of the devil," and he lived with a very visceral fear of "demons taking over his body," he was desperate. The love and peace that Nathan had demonstrated could be experienced through healing felt true to him. It was difficult to deny that God was present in this healing. And truthfully, Daniel had nothing left to lose. It is unfortunate, but all too true, that this is often the place where people need to arrive in their lives in order to seek healing at all costs.

So Daniel came to see us. When Floyd asked what Daniel would like to get out of the session, he spoke of a knot in his chest that he had lived with for a long time. He felt tortured by this knot and said that it made him completely unable to function productively. "I can see it," Floyd answered him. "Would you like to know what it is?"

"Yes," Daniel said. "Very much."

"Let's go find out," Floyd said as he stood up.

We took Daniel up to the treatment room, where he laid down on the mat. We covered him with a blanket, and we placed a blindfold over his eyes to prevent him from being distracted by light or sight.

"You know, man," Floyd began. "All your life, you've been taught not to feel. Today, we're going to feel everything that comes up. You've been told to toughen it up, to be tough. You've been trained that way. Not today."

Floyd instructed Daniel to begin the breathing and, within seconds, the emotion broke through. For Daniel, it felt like an explosion. He began to wail.

"It felt like someone put a knife into my chest and then ripped my chest cavity open, and every emotion in the whole planet, like not just tears but everything—rage and even joy, all in this big bubble—just went boom all at the same time. So you can't say it was tears, because my whole body arched up into the air. I was up on my toes and on my head," Daniel says, remembering the experience.

Daniel continued with the emotional explosion for a while; then it settled down into a heavy grieving. He sobbed for a long time. Floyd encouraged him to let it go and to continue.

Then Floyd said, "Where are you? What do you see? Focus behind your eyes."

"I'm twelve. I'm in the room at home at the moment that I find out that my father has been killed. I had been playing at a friend's house and now my mom is there in tears, and I come walking in. My little sister walks up to me and says 'Dad's dead.' Just straight-faced. She's nine. Everybody's just staring at me. My little sister, she's staring at me."

"She's in shock," Floyd said. "Everybody—they're all in shock." It was then that Daniel described a kind of glass wall growing around him. Suddenly he was unable to see people clearly. They appeared blurry and foggy. The wall grew until it surrounded and encased Daniel.

"You're putting up that wall to protect yourself," Floyd tells Daniel. "It's shifting. Now I'm in the same room with my father. He's at the living room table planning his trip. He's getting up to go."

"Stop him," Floyd said.

Daniel described jumping in front of his father, but being pushed aside.

"Get in front of him. Stop him. Push him."

"I'm grabbing him and pushing him, and he just keeps moving me out of the way," Daniel said.

"Get in front of the door. Block the door!"

Daniel kept trying. He described standing in front of the door and telling his father, "You can't go!" As he did this, he described his father grabbing him and violently slamming him against the wall and heading out the door.

Daniel became very emotionally distraught and shouted, "No!! Don't go! Don't go! You're going to die! This isn't fucking Vietnam!"

"Yes it is," Floyd said. "What?"

"It *is* Vietnam. Your father is still there. He's got a big piece of his spirit still stuck there. And he's on a mission. He's got a death wish. He survived Vietnam, and in his mind, he didn't deserve to survive. His friends died, and he survived. So he's got to give like his friends did." Floyd's own experience as a Vietnam veteran gave him a unique window of understanding into Daniel's father's experience.

Daniel began to see that his father had been caretaking the world. At first he was shocked by this revelation, then he became angry, and then he moved into the type of compassion that comes with healing. He could truly see his father for the first time.

Floyd then got Daniel to his feet. He took the blindfold off so that Daniel could see, then walked Daniel around the room, speaking to him about all of the things his father had missed because of his choices, such as his grandchildren.

Daniel said through sobs, "Yeah, you missed that! You missed it!" Daniel lay down on the mat again, and Floyd put the blindfold back on him. "I want you to call your father to you now," Floyd said.

By that point Daniel was catching on to how the process works, so he quickly responded: "Dad, come here." Daniel's father appeared to him immediately.

"Tell him to look at you," Floyd said. "Look at me, Dad."

"Take his face in your hands."

Floyd brought his face close to Daniel and put his own face in Daniel's hands. Daniel was wearing the blindfold again, so Floyd was simply physically standing in as Daniel's father.

"Look at me," Daniel said. In his mind's eye, Daniel saw his father look at him reluctantly.

"Now speak your truth to him. Whatever is true for you, whatever you really feel," Floyd said.

Daniel began to speak to his father about how he felt about his dad's life choices and how those choices affected him and his family.

Then Floyd said, "Now there's a light opening up behind him.

Do you see it?"

"Yes, I see a door, and it's opening."

"Tell him to go into it. Tell him, 'You've got to go, Dad.'"

Daniel watched in his mind's eye as his father slowly stepped back and moved into the light within the door. Then he was gone, and it went pitch black and cold. Daniel began to tremble.

"Look out into the darkness," Floyd said. "What do you see?" Daniel looked through the door. "It's the twelve-year-old me!

He wants to come home!"

"Try giving him a hug," Floyd suggested.

Daniel reached out to give his twelve-year-old self a hug, and the boy just melted into his body. Daniel felt as though he might pass out. "I feel an intense light inside. Really intense. I just want to stay here and feel that."

After a few moments, Floyd removed the blindfold and helped Daniel to his feet. "Look into my eye; focus on the center of my eye," he said to Daniel. "What do you see?"

Daniel described seeing his father's face smiling widely. "Good. Now he'll be your angel. You can call on him whenever you need him," Floyd said.

After the session, Daniel felt completely transformed. "Everything looked different," he says. "I was just feeling this new skin on my body. The knot was gone, and I felt such an intense peace. I had never felt anything like that before. I felt this openness from my gut."

When Daniel got home, he opened up completely to his wife and told her everything about his pornography addiction and what he'd been feeling. Soon after, his wife had to take a trip with the kids. That gave Daniel the opportunity to stay with his process for a week, working through any feelings that came up; he found that meditating helped. To this day, he says that he meditates every morning to connect with a sense of peace to start his day. When something happens to make him miss his morning meditation, he notices an immediate difference in his stress level.

Now, a few years since Daniel's first experience with RTT, he confidently says, "I'm not an addict anymore."

What Is Addiction?

There are a lot of definitions out there for addiction, but from our perspective at White Raven Center, addiction is the act of running from the self. We are running away from our history, from our shameful experiences, from our guilt. It's fear. It's dishonesty. And it's self-betrayal. It comes from not knowing how to love ourselves. Fundamentally, loving ourselves begins with self-acceptance.

When we're afraid to face the truth about what we feel, we don't accept ourselves. So we try to hide from that lack of self-acceptance through addiction. At the core, addictions are an attempt to fill ourselves up with something outside of us.

The word addiction actually means "without voice"—so it's a state of powerlessness, of lack of authenticity, of not speaking truth. As we become aware of choosing the addiction over our own highest good and the good of those we love, we feel more guilt and self-criticism. Then this pain generated by the addiction drives us back to the addiction. It's a vicious cycle.

Twelve-step programs use the disease model of addiction, based on identifying a physiological source, although more and more rehabilitation centers are now dealing with the underlying emotional issues involved in addiction. Our perspective has no need to dispute the disease model. We simply take it a level deeper by acknowledging that the truth is in the body. Stored within cellular memory is the truth of everything you have ever experienced. Unlike the mind—which is constantly concerned with being right and creating a comfortable, safe version of reality that includes the illusion of control—the body is incapable of lying. It is incapable of experiencing one thing and calling it something else. Only the mind does that.

If, as the disease model would say, there is something akin to an allergic reaction to certain objects of addiction that triggers an uncontrollable and compulsory need for that substance, then we would say that the relationship with that substance, the experiences and feelings born of that relationship, are powerful teachers in that person's journey of self-discovery.

The fact is that alcoholic behavior, for example, doesn't describe addiction; it describes an expression of addiction. Deeper than the possible presence of some physiological response is an inner conflict that would have led the person to some other addiction if it hadn't been alcohol. Our White Raven facilitator Toby Quinn shares: "I have been to many Alcoholics Anonymous meetings where many 'recovering alcoholics' proudly proclaim their liberation from alcohol while chain smoking, eating donut after donut, and drinking five or six cups of coffee within an hour. You can argue that addictions to nicotine, sugar and caffeine are less harmful then addiction to alcohol, but that argument misses the point. Unless we discover what motivates us to look outside ourselves for fulfillment and emotional soothing, we trade one addiction for another and move no closer to the true magnificence and freedom of self-love."

The first step in healing addictions is to acknowledge that we have abandoned ourselves as a result of trauma. Many addictions begin as an unconscious attempt to flee the tyranny of the mind. But for those who have severely rejected themselves, the noise of the rejected soul parts trying to assert themselves and come home can be overwhelming. Addiction can grow out of the desperate attempt to find some relief from this onslaught.

In RTT, addiction is not right or wrong, bad or good. Without the mind's interference and its attempts to control with fear, the body can feel its way back to the source of the self-rejection, release the energy of old wounds, and heal.

As the stories in this chapter illustrate, addiction is—in whatever form it takes—a symptom of emotional trauma and soul loss.

Steven's Story

When Steven experienced some rage that he took out physically on his dog, he realized he needed to do something. He had seen his brother's life radically transformed by RTT, so he decided to try it as well.

"My brother and I both suffered from pretty severe depression and high anxiety," Steven says. "I had started to develop tics, and I'd had butterflies in my stomach for years. I had so much anger. I was never abusive toward my wife physically, but I would rage at her and scream my brains out for a long, long time. Our marriage was incredibly unhealthy. We were hanging on by a thread for years."

It was his second session with Floyd at White Raven Center that Steven says was "epic." In this session, Steven found a young part of his soul lying in the grave with his father, who had died when he was a boy. "My young self was curled up on his side asleep. And I was wearing the same clothes I was wearing the day I found out he had died," he says.

Floyd said, "Hey, you need to wake him up."

So Steven said to the little boy, "Hey, wake up!" But the boy didn't move.

"You've gotta yell louder. You have to find a way to get him out of that grave," Floyd said.

Finally, as Steven commanded his younger self to get up, the boy started to stir and open his eyes. Steven tried to get the boy to come out of the grave, but it was no use. Floyd suggested that Steven get other people to help him, so Steven called on his mother, his brother, and his sisters to help. He saw them all in his mind's eye.

"They were all standing there around the grave, and I'm thinking they're going to help me get him out of the grave," says Steven. "And my mom is just like a statue, and my sisters are just stone cold."

Since that didn't work, Steven decided to try to coax his younger self out of the grave by saying, "Hey, we can play soccer!" That did the trick, and the boy sat up immediately, looking excited. "We'll be on the same team," Steven says. The boy jumped out of the grave and ran toward Steven.

Steven says that it was a powerful moment of acknowledging that he had abandoned this young part of himself. He said to his younger self "I'm here . . . I'm back for you. We'll be together. We'll be on the same team." The grief cracked open his heart at that moment, and Steven began to sob.

Together, they ran to a soccer field near the cemetery that Steven knew of, and Steven began to play soccer with his younger self. "He's having the time of his life. He's laughing," he told Floyd.

After a period of time, Steven heard Floyd's voice say, "Hey, it's time to leave. You need to get him to come with you."

So Steven said to the boy, "Hey, it's time to go. You can come with me now." But the boy just stopped and looked at Steven. "He doesn't want to go," Steven told Floyd.

"Well, he doesn't trust you. You left him here. You abandoned him," Floyd said. "You have to wait for him as long as it takes."

At first, Steven felt very impatient. Eventually, he dropped the impatience and said, "I'll wait for you."

At that moment, the boy leaned his head on Steven's shoulder, drawing Steven's arm around his own small shoulders. "I'll wait as long as I need to," Steven said.

The two watched the sunset together from that soccer field. "The sunset felt like a very intense love," Steven recalls. "It was amazing."

After a while Floyd said, "Okay, it's time to go now. Get down on one knee and look him in the eye. Tell him, 'I'm sorry that I left you, and I know you didn't trust me. But I'm here now, and I see you.'"

Steven repeated Floyd's words and added, "I love you."

Floyd then instructed Steven in how to breathe the boy back into his body. "I watched him turn into kind of a vapor," Steven remembers. "Then I stood there and felt this very powerful feeling in my chest that made me breathe big."

What was the result of Steven's experience with RTT? "My paradigm shifted to this internally driven healing process. I've been freed from addiction. I've been freed from severe depression. I've been freed from massive amounts of anxiety. I've been freed from severe poverty mentalities. I'm taking my life back in ways I could never have dreamed were possible, and to say that I am grateful for this doesn't even come close to what I feel inside almost all of the time."

Lilly's Story

When Lilly first came to us, she was twenty-one years old and immersed in a culture where heavy alcohol use, drugs, and smoking were the norm. She loved to party and get high. She'd been smoking since age eleven, drinking since age twelve, and became sexually active around the same time. Lilly grew up in an environment that allowed her to wander without guidelines or supervision.

The night before she was to come to White Raven Center for the first time, she decided to back out of the workshop. Instead, she got drunk. "I went on a total blackout rampage in my parents' vehicle all through town," Lilly recounts. "Eleven people called the cops on me, and I woke up in jail and thought to myself, 'I hope I didn't kill somebody.' I had a little bit of time in jail to think about what was going on in my life and how if I'd gone to the workshop, I wouldn't have been in jail. So I was definitely more open to the idea of energy work after that." Although Lilly did continue to drink after that experience, she didn't hesitate the next time she had the opportunity to come to White Raven Center and participate in RTT.

Once Lilly started her healing work, she came to realize that for years, she had used substances to numb her emotions and disconnect from her true self. Many of her processing sessions took her back to experiences in her childhood when her older sister repeatedly attempted to kill her.

During an RTT session that I facilitated, one of the memories that came back to Lilly was a drowning attempt. "We were visiting a friend in New Mexico with my parents, and my sister was trying to drown me," she recalls. "She was kind of playing around with me, but she had her hand tangled up in my hair and was aggressively dunking me under the water. She would say stuff to me like 'I'm going to fucking kill you. I'm loco.' I had no idea what that meant back then but later found out that it meant 'I'm crazy' in Spanish. I was terrified, and I screamed for my parents. But we were in this place that was detached from the house, so they couldn't hear me. Then my sister would say, 'It's okay; I was just joking. You're going to be fine. I would never do that to you.' She was five years older than I was, and she would hold me and wait until I'd get nice and calm and my heartbeat would go down. Then she would do it again, and the amount of time she was holding me under the water was getting longer. At one point I just decided, 'Okay, she's going to kill me. There's nothing I can do about it.' I felt that I was in a situation where I just couldn't fight anymore. I was under the water and felt myself go limp."

That trauma led to soul loss for Lilly. "When I processed through this, I realized that was the time where I lost a soul part of myself," she says. "I had to let go to survive because if I'd kept fighting, I think she really would have killed me. As soon as I went limp, she brought me up, and she was crying and freaking out. She said, 'I'm sorry. Please don't tell Mom and Dad.' I watched her eyes go from black to back to being my sister again in that moment."

During RTT, Lilly had a vivid body memory of the experience. "My hands were gnarled, and at one point in the process, I said, 'You guys, I can't move my hands!'" (Gnarling of the hands indicates intense blocked energy stored in the body. The hands relax as soon as the participant connects with repressed truth.)

The soul retrieval experience after this memory was very profound for Lilly. "As soon as I brought that little girl back into my body and reassured her that she's safe now in this body and that it's time to come home, that nobody is trying to hurt her, there's no evil sister trying to drown her, she came in. It was like I felt her enter into my body. I felt the energy flow. It was like this huge missing piece that really didn't trust people came back, and it was like I started a new life that day. I felt light, really light. When you call the soul part in, you can feel the energy just flowing all the way in to fill up your whole body, and you get this kind of euphoric feeling. You're being reunited with the part of yourself that you haven't seen or recognized in a long time, which is amazing."

Once her soul part returned, Lilly re-experienced her adventurous spirit at that age. This soul part immediately said, "I want a snake and a lizard as pets," and Lilly remembered that she had loved reptiles as a girl. She was able to access her child energy again, which has allowed her to be more playful with her own young daughter. "One of the things I really enjoyed as a kid was lying on the bed while my mom was fixing it and letting the blankets fall onto me really slowly. Before [RTT], I didn't really have much patience with my daughter when she wanted to do that, but after doing the work, I realized, 'Wait a minute! I really loved that as a kid, too!'"

Lilly had many more processes that involved her sister's abuse. "There were a lot of instances where she would hold me under blankets," Lilly says. "When I was a five-year-old, she would tell me, 'I'm going to hold you in here forever. You're never going to get out.' As a five-year-old, I would believe her and freak out. I would think, 'Oh my God, I can't breathe!' I would feel stuck in there forever. A lot of the processes that I do, I go back to that, and I'm right there again underneath the blankets fighting for my life, screaming and crying for somebody to save me. Usually that's followed by bringing soul parts back, too."

Because of what happened to her in her childhood, Lilly never showed her emotions. Instead, she immediately grabbed a cigarette or a drink when her feelings threatened to come to the surface. "When I actually faced those emotions and allowed myself to feel and figure out where the feelings were coming from, I could remove them so that I could consciously make decisions," she says. "I would get a pull that I really want to go out tonight. I want to go drink. And then, I would be able to sit down and say, 'Okay, where is this coming from? Why do I feel this way?' And I was able to get in tune with my body and figure out why it was that I was wanting to go out. A lot of the times, it would be stress from my family."

Lilly feels that she would never have been able to cultivate the strong sense of family she has in her life today, or enjoy the beauty of her family relationships, if she hadn't reconnected with the lost parts of her soul. She says that RTT connected her to loving herself in a way she never knew existed.

"After years of abuse and bad experiences, it really hardened who I was. My personality was always on guard and cautious and probably not very pleasant to be around," Lilly shares. "After the energy work and bringing these soul parts back, I was able to connect with who I am and who I was and find these greater qualities like my love for treats and playing, and that sort of thing, and bring them back into my life and share them with my family."

Aaron's Story

When Aaron first came to White Raven Center, he came to interview us in a professional and matter-of-fact manner. It felt to Floyd and me like he was interviewing us for a job. Aaron was smiling and appeared lighthearted as he sat on a kitchen stool asking us questions. At the time, little did we know the extent of his addiction and his childhood trauma. Aaron was a master performer, a true wordsmith, and a college graduate with a law degree. He hid well the underlying truth that he was suicidal and close to death as a result of his heavy use of alcohol and drugs.

Once Aaron began processing at WRC, we learned from him the full extent of his childhood trauma. He was raised in a rough and tough environment in an Alaskan logging camp, which was full of men whose lives were characterized by violence and alcohol. Aaron's dad was the manager of the camp. As a little boy, Aaron felt unbearable pressure to fit in and witnessed horrendous acts of violence, both accidental and intentional. Aaron was not allowed to show any signs of weakness or emotion, or he would be severely reprimanded.

The following story reflects a time in Aaron's childhood that was supposed to be a coming of age ritual, signifying transition from boyhood into young adulthood. Aaron knew that the tacit expectation was to shoot a buck. Instead, the experience reflects the oppression of a young boy who so desperately wanted to please his father.

"When I began the process in my breathing, I immediately went back to a traumatic event in my life, and that was when I killed a doe as a ten-year-old boy," he recalls. While processing, the memories came back for Aaron very vividly. It was as if he were re-experiencing it. "I could see the thin layer of snow on the ground and how the tracks burned through it to the forest floor. I could smell the gunpowder in the air, I could hear my ears ringing from the muzzle blast, and I could see that the doe was struggling down there below me. I went right back into it in a way that I could never have the bravery to do if I wasn't in a circle of people caring for me."

During RTT, Aaron vividly re-experienced the feelings he felt that day. "Those feelings were fear—fear not only of a dying animal but also my own fear of not doing well because in the culture I was raised in, this was a really important event. So there was fear of disappointing my dad and my elders. It was really a high-pressure event for a young boy in my culture," Aaron says, talking about the expectations placed on boys in the male- dominant environment in which he grew up.

"I originally shot at her and missed, and the deer all ran off. We ran up on top of this hill, and my dad with his deer whistle started calling, and this doe came back," he says. "When she got within range I shot her right through the heart, and the bullet went up and broke her backbone. She was making this horrible, horrible sound and struggling, pulling herself up on the snow with her two front legs with her eyes big and wide with fear. We went running down there, and I immediately just burst into tears. I was just mortified that this living, beautiful thing was in such pain, and I had caused it. It was the worst nightmare you could imagine. And so my dad had me look away, and he shot the doe in the head. Then we gutted out the deer, and my dad put her on his back and cut off the head because it was all exploded from getting shot at close range."

When they walked back to their camp, Aaron, as this young boy, was filled with horror that he had taken a life. "Not only had I done something horrible, I had failed in this rite of passage by crying and being upset, which was really looked down upon.

Shame—incredible shame—because I failed. So it was kind of a double-edged sword for me. I felt bad, and I felt bad for feeling bad. And by bad, I mean the very worst feeling you can have," he says. As a result of this experience, Aaron says he always believed that he wouldn't be able to perform well at anything.

In his emotional processing session, Aaron went deeply into the shame and experienced it fully. "On the other side of the shame, I was able to see the truth that it wasn't all that shameful," he says. "Maybe it was human. I was able to go so deep into it and move those feelings by engaging with them. And in doing so, I saw that things were not as I had imagined them as a boy. There was more to what was happening than I could understand from that vantage point of my life. I was able to look at this transformative event in my life from a place of wisdom and adulthood. I could see the event taking place again with all of the sensational reality of it, with all of it just like it was happening at that time, only I saw a new truth—a truth that had been there all along. And that was that this deer was coming back into my life to save me and that this experience was, instead of life-damaging, actually life-saving and ultimately redemptive."

I asked Aaron to explain how it was redemptive. He shared that he was able to turn the traumatic event into what he calls "a beautiful myth—a guiding star to live by." While processing, Aaron had a vision of a deer-woman holding him as a little boy— the soul part of him who had been trapped in that time. "She took care of me as if she'd been waiting for the sacred day when I would revisit the trauma and the gun smoke and the horrible dying sounds to claim what was my birthright, which is to be a loving and sensitive human being," Aaron says. "Not being able to take on the mantle that I wanted so badly of the perfect man that kills without remorse, I was unable to become that. And instead, this deer—dying like she did—in that instant saved my soul from the way that I was supposed to go, that I was being acculturated in."

This process was a very powerful soul retrieval experience for Aaron. "I saw a part of myself that really hadn't been part of life but was stuck in this wounded place, stuck in the forest," he says. "What happens in these traumatic events is that part of us gets alienated from the world. Through the soul retrieval process, when the myth has become resonant again with life instead of this backwater of pain and suffering, all of a sudden, you have one of these moments where it all makes sense, where you can believe again that everything happens for a reason. It's so amazingly redemptive to have this horrible suffering become a myth of power. When we're wounded, it becomes cold, but in the heart of the wound is the gold."

What Aaron experienced is something that we refer to as a "partial life review"—a powerful core emotional process that gives us a snapshot of our life and shows how, like a spiderweb, our life is woven together. Suddenly it all makes sense. We experience a flooding of wisdom, a conscious knowledge of the purpose behind the relationships and/or experiences that served as the reflections of fragmented soul pieces.

By taking responsibility for our suffering and by allowing ourselves to fully feel our feelings instead of blaming them on somebody or something else, the purpose of our suffering is revealed to us. We recognize that we have been trapped in a cycle of illusions that no longer serve us. We recognize that we have been living in a self-imposed prison through our belief that nothing will ever change. It is one of those "Aha!" moments that shows us that what we have been looking for our whole lives has been right there inside of us all along. We have a shift in perspective and a new level of awareness and consciousness that allows us to live life from a place of nurturing our souls. The partial life review aids us in this revelation, facilitating our acceptance that the trauma did happen but isn't happening anymore.

So, how did this experience change Aaron? "When I look back on my past, it was like I was looking at TV. Now it's like I see the world in high definition," he says. "The work has transformed the way that I see the world and my place in it. It's life-changing. I tell people to watch out because once you do the work, your life will change in ways that you can't imagine . . . and dramatically."

Aaron no longer struggles with alcoholism, and his life has transformed in terms of work, relationships, health and general well-being. Aaron is now the loving father of two incredible and extremely intelligent children. He and his beautiful wife continue to grow and evolve together.

Michael's Story

Like Daniel and Steven, Michael struggled with an addiction to pornography. "I was raised in a Christian household, and I found that many of my fellow men that were raised in that household struggled with porn addiction," Michael says.

"I was raised by hardline Southern Baptist Christian parents, and I knew that didn't work for me as a worldview or in my experience for society as a whole. Steven had told me that RTT is really intense work, and I'm an adventurer. I'm a mariner, I'm a mountaineer, I'm an adrenaline junkie. I was afraid, but at the same time, I was fearless. It didn't feel cultish in a sense that there was going to be some mastermind guru that I had to do what they say, or where I was going to lose myself."

Michael describes his first processing experience as uncomfortable, but it was still fruitful. In his second processing session during the weekend, he worked with Floyd. He found himself back in his parents' house when he was a boy.

"I went back to the crib that my parents would lock me in, and I felt the crib. I saw the wallpaper on the wall. I went back to that place for real—not just in the memory, but it was tangible. In that process, I realized that my parents had abandoned me as a child, starting from a very young age, because in the memory of that experience and of reliving it with my adult mind, I was alone, the lights were off, the door was shut, and no one was answering my cries," he says.

"Interestingly enough, that matched with what my mother has told me about that time. In her marriage to my father, he was at sea in the US Navy, and she had three little kids to care for. She didn't know how to take care of herself, so she couldn't take care of us. She would just lock me in the room."

In his process, Michael could finally give his infant self a voice and express what he felt about being abandoned. "I got really upset at my mom in the process, which has always been hard for me in real life," he says. "But in that process, I learned how to have a voice in speaking to my mother. After that weekend, I no longer have a problem saying, 'Mom, here's how I feel, and you can deal with it however you will, but this is how I feel.'"

Next in his process, Michael found himself moving in his memory to a couple of years later. He was in the same house, in bunk beds that he shared with his brother. He was afraid to go to the bathroom at night, fearing that there were monsters under his bed. "Floyd led me into doing hand-to-hand combat with these monsters. I could see them in my mind, and in the process, I was physically acting out the battle with a wiffle ball bat and a pillow and some bedsheets. I acted out killing those monsters that used to terrify me at night. Thus I gained power over those demons," he says.

Then he had a vision of a beautiful homestead surrounded by bright green power lines, like Star Wars-type energy fields. He kicked all of the monsters out and said, "You can't be around here anymore." "I realized that I wet the bed when I was a child because I was so miserable in my existence and didn't have anything to contain my experience. I realized that I would fall asleep so intensely at night that I would leave myself and disconnect from my body," he says. "So it was no big deal if my body said it was time to urinate.

I would just pee and not even wake up."

In a further process during the weekend workshop, Michael and his fiancée worked together as a couple. "I wouldn't say it saved our relationship," he says, "but it allowed our relationship to progress forward while previous to going there, there was no hope of it progressing. It allowed my fiancée to feel safe with me. That's powerful. It introduced a new level of trust and intimacy that was not there before."

That first weekend was exceptionally transforming for Michael. "I can't explain it, but I've been less stressed out, and I've had a way easier time in every relationship of my life since that really intense process. I faced dangerous things that day with my own strength and Floyd's leadership, and I killed some demons and pushed them out of my reality. You can put whatever words on it you want, but that's what happened. It doesn't really matter, because what matters is the experience itself, and there just aren't words for what happens in that space. I don't feel that there's anything absolute in my experiences. I'm just trying to convey my experience so that other people might get some idea of what it was like."

After some time following the workshop, Michael found himself feeling anxious and struggling with insomnia, as well as smoking a lot of marijuana. He was unable to shake it, so he had a phone session with Floyd. "The process I had on the phone was just as powerful as my epic session I had with Floyd in person. I ended up working on being bullied in high school and being molested as a teenager by one of my friends," he says. "And I did more work around my family, and holy cow, I have felt a lightness since then. I have felt a new centeredness. I've had an easier time at work. I've had an easier time in all my relationships. I went back home on Father's Day with my family there for the first family meeting in three years, and it was okay."

Michael shares truth with me that he still struggles a bit with his addiction, yet it is completely different now. "From thirteen to twenty-eight, I was unconsciously addicted to pornography and sexual fantasy. I still feel it tugging at me, but I was hopelessly addicted before. Now I'm struggling. But I know what I need to do to get better, and I'm doing it. That changes everything. I am empowered to control my own destiny, and in my darkest places when I'm having the hardest time and I'm really struggling, if I close my eyes and take a couple deep breaths and visualize the experience of breathing my spirit back in, whatever you want to call it, I have the power to break the pull of the addiction. That is life-changing. Having power over the addiction instead of it having power over me—that's what happens. I'm so glad that I've embarked on this path because I'm a lot happier than I used to be. I'm wildly, powerfully, intimately free to be myself."

Michael has changed his occupation as well, in just one year after coming to White Raven Center. "I went from a hands-on worker to a made man in my industry," he says. "So it changed my life with my family, with my addiction, with my most intimate relationships, occupationally, my worldview, and my spirit. Everything is different in this better way. I can't even explain it. I can't say I'm in heaven all the time. I still struggle, but my life is radically transformed."

Cathy's Story

While conducting a research project involving Alaska Native women who suffered from domestic violence, I met Cathy, who was providing wellness counseling in a village near where she grew up. The village had been deeply affected by addiction, and Cathy's childhood was unstable and unpredictable as a result. She was often neglected and isolated from others, and when adults were around, the experience was not positive a lot of the time. "I saw a lot of violence—fistfights, knife fights and things like that, which were always alcohol-related," she says.

At the time I met Cathy, she was experiencing a huge amount of body pain and looked fatigued and aged well beyond her twenty- eight years. I encouraged her to consider participating in the RTT process offered at the White Raven Center.

Cathy shared with me that she spent a lot of time intoxicated when she was just four and five years old. "So many of my memories from that time frame were very fuzzy, like looking back into a time when you were drinking, except for that I was a very little kid. Learning how to drink at such a young age and continuing to do that up until my early twenties had a lot of trauma associated with it," she says.

Eventually, Cathy did come in to our center and in one of her processes, she experienced a soul retrieval of little girl parts of herself. "When those parts came home, I was talking for a few minutes like I was intoxicated, and I was feeling it throughout my entire body," she says.

"As I brought those soul pieces back that had been shattered, there was an integration process that lasted a few hours. And I was feeling like a little kid for a while there, which is why White Raven is so important, because they provide that safety where you're protected while you're bringing those parts home. The people in charge, what I refer to as spirit watchers, are keeping track of what's happening and keeping you safe. I had a lot of physical and emotional little girl feelings that came back. Then, of course, they settle out and integrate after a short period of time, and there's a feeling of being full—a feeling of being more connected to the planet."

How has Cathy's life changed as a result of her RTT work? "I'm excited about whatever is going on in front of me now and not worried about the past. Not thinking about the future so much, enjoying right now," she says. "I'm the one that shuts off her cell phone for four days and goes off hiking. That's all stuff I would have been afraid to do before. I'm no longer looking for another person to help me find my bliss each moment of each day. Rather, I seek my bliss each day through my spiritual, emotional, mental and physical journey in this life. The journey that I have taken through this process has been a challenging and delightful one that continues to grow and change with each day. I feel strong, powerful, and full of love for all the people of the world that I am blessed to come into contact with. I feel connected to the universe. I am not alone."

Cathy has experienced many years of healing through the RTT process. She found the confidence to complete her master's and doctorate degrees, and today she is an amazing facilitator of the RTT process and member of the WRC team.

"Rescuing and caretaking
mean almost
what they sound like.
We rescue people from their
responsibilities.
We take care of people's
responsibilities for them.
Later we get mad at them
for what we've done.
Then we feel used
and sorry for ourselves.
This is the pattern, the triangle."

—Melody Beattie

Chapter 7

Caretakers Discover the Benefits of RTT

Caretaking is a topic we discuss extensively in our White Raven weekend sessions. The majority of our participants raise their hands when we ask the question, "Who in this room is a caretaker?" All of us who are facilitators—Floyd, me, Toby, Rebecca (whose story you will read shortly), Cathy, and others—were groomed to take care of other people. This is not necessarily a bad thing. The issue here is that it becomes out of balance. When we become obsessed with caring for others and routinely neglect care for ourselves, we perpetuate unhealthy patterns and create increased suffering. As I learned from Native elders, all things in the universe are part of a system that strives to be in balance.

We have seen several clients who are so obsessed with "saving the world" that they just can't do enough. As a result, they find themselves carrying a heavy burden of guilt. When a tragedy occurs anywhere in the world, they take it personally and feel responsible. They feel the need to do something, to fix it, and the guilt builds from the frustration of not knowing what to do. This is caretaking in one of its most extreme forms.

Shifting this dynamic to the family, we may become enmeshed in the suffering of those we love. As a result we neglect our own needs, our own wants, and our own desires. We enter a failure mode and get stuck in a cycle of "no matter what I do, it is never going to be enough."

Who Is the Caretaker?

At first glance, most people would probably identify the characteristics of a caretaker as positive. In fact, many caretakers find it hard to change their patterns because of how much positive attention they get for their constant attending to other people's needs. On the surface, caretakers are givers—they do indeed deeply care. They are often sensitive, compassionate, empathic, and intuitive deep-feelers who are good listeners and problem- solvers. They usually value these qualities in themselves and come to rely on the praise and acknowledgment from friends, family and colleagues for being such "strong, selfless people." Social service agencies love this type of person, because they give and give and give. They are treated like heroes, and this propels them to do more. After years of giving unconditionally, they become exhausted and frequently depressed. Depression occurs when we deny ourselves full truth and repress our emotions.

In addition to caretaking family and friends, they may be drawn to professional work in the areas of counseling, social work, or social and environmental activism. Basically, they feel the noble call to help others. So, why would such a person need healing?

The answer is that the deeper and often subconscious motivation for these "selfless" behaviors is often a denial of self. Especially when the caretaker gives to the point of self-denial, the individual gives in order to escape repressed feelings that they are failing. It's much easier to focus attention on another's problems than to face the truth of our relationship with ourselves. Focusing on others offers a very powerful distraction from our own feelings.

Caretakers will, in martyr-like fashion, regularly sacrifice and compromise their own self-care and nurturing in order to attend to the needs of others. In this way, caretaking can be thought of as an addiction.

The caretaker betrays the self, and this self-sacrifice often has roots in an exaggerated sense of responsibility for other people. It's common for deeply sensitive, compassionate, and empathic people to tune into the feelings of others to the extent that they actually feel at fault for the pain of others. For example, people who have been abused may feel especially sensitive to others who have been abused. To compensate for the pain within, the caretaker will take on the other person's fears, concerns, worries and phobias and make it a mission to alleviate that person's suffering. On the surface, this is a beautiful intention. However, because the underlying motivation is to escape the feelings connected to the caretaker's own experience with abandonment, what's really happening is a form of emotional escapism.

The other likely outcome of this relationship is that the caretaker will eventually become resentful of the person he/she has tried to save. The truth is that we only have the power to heal ourselves, so the caretaker will give a tremendous amount of energy to this other person only to discover that nothing changes. The caretaker is then left with the feeling that he/she loves and cares for everybody else while nobody cares for him/her. Ultimately, this is only a projection of the caretaker's own lack of self-love.

We must acknowledge, honor, and ultimately accept our own feelings if we are to heal. When we focus on and take responsibility for another person's feelings, all that happens is that the one being "saved" becomes dependent on the caretaker and is stripped of the opportunity to develop the capacity to heal on their own. The caretaker, in turn, resents the dependency and is unaware that he/she created it.

This leaves the caretaker feeling like a victim to his/her perceived moral obligation and compulsion to focus on others, which leads to self-pity. Eventually, due to the likely presence of shame, guilt, and strong self-judgment, the caretaker will judge all of those feelings and end up looking for someone else to care for in an attempt to stuff down those feelings. Then the cycle begins again. For the caretaker, the RTT process might uncover feelings of being undeserving of the self-attention that is necessary to heal. The caretaker may be very resistant to caring for self, saying "I'm fine. What about everybody else?" Over the years at several of our workshops, we have had participants choose to leave the session after listening to each person's check-in on Friday evening. They compare their own lives to the shared experiences of other participants and deem their own suffering to be unworthy of being a part of the circle. In these instances, the group as a whole holds no judgment toward the person choosing to leave. Those who stay discover that there is more pain underlying their need to help others than they realized.

RTT dissolves the illusion that fixing others creates control and power. The caretaker begins to see that he/she has been uncomfortable with allowing others to feel their feelings, to the same extent that he/she has been afraid to feel his/her own feelings.

Many of our clients find that caretaking behavior shifts as a natural byproduct of RTT. For example, Cathy says she was wrapped up in codependent/caretaking behaviors with most of her family and friends. "As I did the work through RTT," she says, "I released those negative behaviors because I let go of the root of the problem—my neediness, my dependency, my fear. As the fear went away I didn't need the behavior anymore, and I set myself free through understanding the process of releasing emotional energy. I didn't need to be attached to negative fear energies."

Leah's Story

Leah says that her whole life, she had been a caretaker showing up for others but never sure how to do the same for herself. "I wasn't conscious that I was holding trauma. I'd done healing work before, but I hadn't really claimed my own wounding. I wanted to be in a healing space because I wanted to learn how to heal other people. I didn't realize that I had my own work to do first," she says.

Her first workshop was an eye-opener. "People started sharing at White Raven, and I realized that I had to be real and that I didn't necessarily know what my 'real' was," she says. "I got scared. I wasn't clear how to be in my body. There was so much self-judgment about not knowing what I was 'supposed' to be doing. People expressed their trauma and were being loved in that. People were unloading and crying. I wanted to analyze and understand, and when it came to be my turn, there was again this idea that there was a 'right' way to do it. Of course, I wanted to do it 'the right way.'"

It took quite a while for Leah to let go and allow the feelings to emerge with the breath. As the resistance melted, she discovered many things about herself. "I am so much more than I ever really felt like I was," she says.

Unlike many of the people who come to White Raven Center, Leah can't pinpoint a specific traumatic event that led to her issues. From an objective standpoint, she had an easy childhood. Nevertheless, society taught her not to feel. When she began RTT, she found frustration and anger toward herself, as well as rage toward her parents, and a great deal of codependent/caretaking behavior.

She thinks of RTT as sort of like a virus-clearing software program. "You can't leave the viruses on the computer. You can pretend they aren't there, but eventually, they're going to destroy things." It's the same with our emotions, she says. "We get all this spam in our lives. Report the spam, and unsubscribe to the negative email lists! Identify the virus programs, clear out your inbox, and reinstall the appropriate things that you choose to live by," she says.

Leah also uses the analogy of a search engine. "Just like Google, when you search for the word 'wrong,' that's what you're going to find. It's the program you run when you get up in the morning." In other words, if you look for what's wrong in your life, that's what you will find. "Be conscious of what you put in that search box in the morning," Leah says. "'Gratitude' is a good one."

Today, Leah finds that she is much less likely to take care of others from a compulsive place, and she has learned how to better care for herself.

Lilly's Story

Lilly, who lived through years of abuse from her sister, discovered through RTT work that she was completely enmeshed with her family. "I imagined myself in this spiderweb with my family, and I was stuck there," she says. "I was totally bound. And to move the energy, I had to cut all the strings around me. I had to cut myself out of the web."

Lilly began to notice how often she denied her own needs in deference to the needs of her family. "I remember I called my sister one time after this beautiful camping trip where I saw trumpeter swans and heard wolves howling. I called her because I wanted to share that with her, and she said, 'I found out my babysitter is addicted to crack.'" Lilly immediately shifted from her own experience and focused on her sister's problem.

The enmeshment with her family affected Lilly's relationship with her husband as well. After moving enough energy through RTT, she came to a realization. "If I want to be present for myself, for my husband, and for my children, I can't let any of this negative stuff from my family into my life because it's not mine to carry. I've got to protect myself, and

I've got to set boundaries. In my family, the family rule was [that] there were no boundaries. Children were allowed in the room when the adults were discussing adult affairs, if you can imagine that," she says.

Setting boundaries was painful at times because Lilly's family did not want her to change, and they became angry and directed their anger at her. Lilly had become protective of the family she had created with her husband and children. "Sometimes, I have to tell my parents and sister, 'Listen, guys, this is what I need to do to protect *my* family, and I'm really sorry that it offends you. But that's just the way it is.' That's been difficult, but it's been good because I really feel like my children are the beneficiaries and so am I."

Lilly's story shows us the powerful transformation that can occur when the caretaker switches focus from caretaking others to taking care of herself.

Renee's Story

"I wasn't too interested in core emotional processing when I first went to White Raven Center. I was more accustomed to 'sit and talk' counseling sessions that were brief and didn't get to the core of anything," Renee says. "I resisted feeling my feelings because my mind erroneously told me I didn't need the help. However, the body never lies. My body tried to tell me this truth for several years, but I ignored every sign and symptom as just being a physical ailment instead of acknowledging that my stress and bottled up feelings were part of what was being manifested. For a long time, I didn't know how to tap into emotions of abandonment, anger, rage, self-hate, fear, grief, trauma, and pain."

Renee's first experience with RTT was in a phone appointment with Floyd. She had witnessed an accident in which a little boy was hit by a car, and she had repeated traumatic flashbacks as a result. After one experience of RTT processing, Renee says that she had no more flashbacks.

It was when she attended a workshop, however, that she really began to see a difference in herself. She had been to both individual and couples counseling before, but she only touched the surface of her emotions in those sessions. "When I went to an RTT workshop, and I was witnessing other people, I felt like I had permission to let myself go there," Renee says. "That's when I finally started really getting into what I needed to discharge."

"A big part of why I wanted to do this work was for my kids," she goes on. "I had this anger that was out of control, and I'd blow up at them and yell. I didn't like feeling like a monster, and I didn't understand why I couldn't control it. I had so much anger, fear, just darkness—it felt like black sludge almost. It felt like it wasn't me. But I think they've noticed a big difference in me. Whenever I would go back home after a workshop, especially my oldest— she's more emotionally in tune—she would just hug me and hug me. It felt so good to feel this good energy between us."

When her daughter turned four, Renee found herself especially triggered. This is because when Renee was four years old, she experienced serious trauma that caused her to create an imaginary friend. She didn't remember this friend but was told about it by her grandmother. Then, in an RTT session, the memories flooded back.

"This imaginary friend was taking on all the bad feelings I had from being hurt," Renee says. "I'd be in my room all by myself. My parents would be out drinking and drugging, and I would organize my room and clean it. And then I'd destroy it. Then I'd organize it and clean it again. It was something to do so that I wasn't thinking and worried about where my parents were. When are they going to be here? Why am I by myself? All that fear that I was experiencing."

It was only through RTT processing that Renee recalled her experiences of being left alone by her parents when she was a toddler. Her parents' addiction was the biggest source of childhood pain for her. "When my mom was sober, I felt this love and connection and bond. Everything was great, and then gone!" Renee recalls. "There was nothing I could do to keep her with me, and I did everything I could. I was one of the little star people in school, the do-gooder. I did everything to try to make her happy, and then I would feel like a failure when I didn't." This is when Renee's caretaking behaviors took hold.

Now, Renee and her husband both participate in RTT. "There have been a couple of times when my husband and I have witnessed each other's processes. We talked about how we were triggering each other and how we were perfect mirrors for each other," Renee says.

"My husband is a perfect mirror for triggering me, based on my childhood experiences, and I was his perfect triggermate. We would get into arguments, and he'd want to leave and walk out the door. And I'd feel abandoned. There would be times when he'd want to leave, and I wouldn't let him," Renee says. RTT helped her recognize and understand how she was triggering her husband by not allowing him to go when he needed space. Sometimes, she lets him leave and deals with her discomfort of feeling abandoned, and sometimes, he stays and deals with his discomfort as he talks with her.

"I feel like I've been blessed to have a husband who has also done his work. We can connect in that way and understand why it's so important and support each other. It's helped us with our kids. We have become a really strong team," she says.

Her toddler-aged children have also done sessions with us at White Raven Center. Working with children is a different experience. They are usually more emotionally accessible than adults and can often easily release emotional traumas before they become "stuck" energy.

As a result of processing with RTT, Renee's anger has been significantly diminished. When she does get angry, she can observe herself. If the energy is intense, she can find a safe avenue to release it that is not focused on her children. Renee has learned to remind herself that it's just a feeling passing through her. She can also now tell when her heart is open or closed, and she can consciously open it if she wants to. "Usually, if it's closed, it means there's something I need to process," she says. "And I'm still learning how to maintain it being open. I'm still amazed and flabbergasted by the difference I've seen in myself."

"It wasn't until I went to a workshop that I started to give myself permission to fully release the pockets of energy that were stuck and consuming my life. I had become a master of numbing out and escaping my own body to avoid feeling pain. Now I embrace the pain," she says. "I welcome the opportunity to feel what I previously thought I couldn't survive. I accept my truth, and I'm not afraid. As I unpacked loads and loads of emotional sludge, I made room for the love and light. I have gone through a tremendous transformation, and energy is still shifting. As my energy has shifted, my relationships have greatly improved. My heart is open to myself and others. I see life differently. I feel hopeful and alive."

"My prayer for all of our relations, our communities, our world, is for this healing and inner peace to be seen as something that is within everyone's grasp," Renee continues. "We are all connected. As I have heard said many times at White Raven Center, 'When we heal ourselves, we heal the world.' This is making more and more sense every day. Life is a beautiful gift, and we are a work in progress. I am very grateful for this healing journey, and as a keychain that I have says, 'The healing journey continues.'"

Setting the Stage for Caretaking With Soul Exchange

Children may be conditioned early on to be caretakers, as a way of gaining attention and approval from the adults in their lives. Some parents are so obsessed with controlling their children that they unconsciously train them to discount their own value. The unspoken agreements that are fundamental to this "training" may result in what we sometimes refer to as soul exchange. For example, an agreement between a parent and a child might be: "I will take care of you if you will love me."

A child being cared for under such an agreement/exchange might absorb part of a parent's soul to the point that the child acts, talks, feels, and thinks just like the parent. In exchange, the parent holds a part of the child's soul for the purpose of filling up an empty space in the parent, due to his/her own unconscious soul loss. This is a spell that can be broken—if healing is to occur, it must be broken! Otherwise, with soul exchanges, each person is interfering with the other's experience of life.

What are some of the ways that parents create soul exchanges with their children? A subtle form might be when a depressed mother talks to her child as if he/she were her counselor. The child may feel special in that moment, considering that "for once, I matter." A more overt way of training a child to be a caretaker is when the child is beaten if he/she doesn't prepare dinner for the younger siblings. Getting trapped in a caretaking role usually means giving up the opportunity to play, to be creative—in short, to have a childhood.

These children become responsible little adults. They give their souls away to their parents because they want to help, even if it means repeatedly sacrificing their own needs for love and attention. They have learned not to trust others or have expectations of them. Instead, they try to get their needs met vicariously through taking care of others. It becomes a way to receive some sense of approval. It's a form of conditioned love, yet not the care and nurturing they deserve.

Caretaking children do not have a strong sense of self. They look to external sources for validation—for example, to find joy in the eyes of their parent. They translate this to "I'm happy, too!" These children serve as little sponges, taking on the pain, suffering, grief, and even anger that is not fully or appropriately expressed by their parents or other adult caretakers. This is especially the case for children raised by emotionally detached parents.

During RTT sessions, we sometimes work with clients on severing these caretaking roles and damaging soul agreements. That's what happened for Claire, whose partial story was first mentioned in chapter 2, and who had a particularly enmeshed relationship with her father. Even though her dad is deceased, she found herself screaming at him in her RTT session, angry about all he expected her to give him while he was alive. Toby, who was facilitating that particular session, seized the moment to help Claire let go of the soul exchange that she had unconsciously created with her father.

Toby instructed Claire to tell her father that she was giving him back responsibility for himself. "I'm not your parent! I'm not taking care of you anymore! I'm not taking on your feelings! Take them back. It's your responsibility to take care of you now. I'm giving it all back to you!" she shouted.

Then Toby instructed her to physically feel all that she had taken on from her father, gathered in her hands. On the count of three, she threw everything she'd taken on back to her dad. This experience helped her to break the contract that resulted in soul exchange, and to restore to balance her caretaking behavior. Claire continues to work on her caretaker addiction with her relationship with her brother. Releasing the energy connected deeply to the experience with her father has supported this effort.

Restoring Balance

Caretakers have a powerful and important role in society, and we in no way want to downplay that fact. There is nothing wrong with helping others; however, we need to ask ourselves what motivates our desire to help. For those who are constantly taking care of others, a caretaker addiction is most likely present, and RTT can help to dislodge the need to project care onto others, instead teaching you to bring that care back to the self where it belongs.

Then the caregiving person can give from a place that's clear and true—rather than from an inner need that is not being fulfilled by the self. The giving is healthy and free of agenda, because the person is also giving to himself/herself in a healthy way. Balance has returned.

"Psychology traditionally approached trauma
through its effects on the mind.
This is at best only half the story and a wholly
inadequate one. Without the body
and mind accessed together as a unit,
we will not be able to deeply understand
or heal trauma."

—Peter A. Levine

Chapter 8

Physical Symptoms Shift and Heal

"A friend of mine told me that her sister had an operation because of stomach pain, only for the surgeons to discover there was nothing visibly wrong," Floyd shared with our White Raven team one day. "Experiencing pain in another part of her stomach, she chose to have yet another operation, only for the doctors to discover a healthy functioning organ." This is an example of how emotional energy stored in the body can manifest into experiences that feel physical.

We know that emotional energy related to traumas experienced within the family tends to be stored in the region of the belly. In the family of the woman with the stomach issues, the father was emotionally silent. He was detached and basically did not share anything. The mother was addicted to pharmaceutical drugs and remained emotionally absent. The message in the family was "don't feel."

When we don't feel our emotions, they can manifest as pain in the body. Energy blocks interfere with the body's natural energetic flow. This leads to all forms of disease. The body is designed to move energy, to keep it flowing. When the energy of emotions becomes stagnant and repressed, we create disease—literal dis-ease—in the body. After witnessing thousands of client sessions, our experiences at the White Raven Center tell us that most ailments of the body can be diminished, even fully corrected, when the related emotional energy blocks are moved.

We would never say that all physical problems can be solved by RTT or any type of emotional processing. However, in our experience, the vast majority of physical issues do respond positively to this type of work. The personal experiences shared in this chapter will demonstrate how the emotional body and the physical body are connected. Releasing the energy of emotional trauma and experiencing soul retrieval can facilitate the resolution of physical suffering. We each have the resources within ourselves to restore our body's natural capacity to heal itself. We have witnessed this phenomenon time and again.

Stormy's Story

I first met Stormy in a dance class I was taking at the Alaska Club. Chatting in the locker room after class and observing her behavior, I noticed that Stormy grimaced when she moved her shoulder. She shared with me that she was experiencing intense pain and was fearful that she would have to give up her beloved dancing. Half-jokingly, I said, "Why don't you come to White Raven Center, and we will fix that shoulder problem of yours." Eventually, motivated by her pain, Stormy decided to take me up on the offer.

The following story is an example of the cruelty that can and does happen to children. Despite the incredibly painful experiences Stormy endured, she became a dance instructor, is successful in her career, raised three children with love, and owns her own home. Stormy's story is one of courage and perseverance, and it clearly demonstrates the power of the human spirit to heal.

"The first few hours at the workshop, I was kinda freaked out," Stormy recalls. "I didn't understand what the workshop

Physical Symptoms Shift and Heal

was truly about. I just wanted to heal my arm. All of a sudden, the person on the floor who was processing jumped up and was swinging a bat and chasing Floyd around the room. I was shocked by the rage that was being expressed and felt terrified. I backed up against the wall and watched, and I seriously thought about leaving. 'I don't have that kind of anger in me,' I thought. But I was assured that everyone processes differently. Not all processes were big and involved swinging a bat."

Stormy admits that she had few memories of her childhood. She didn't recall, for example, that her father had sexually abused her. "As an adult, I thought my dad was a really strong parent and that he really loved me a lot."

When she lay on the mat and began the breathing, "A horrible memory came back. And it was like I was living through it and watched it all over again as a very, very little child," she says. "One of the nightmares that I used to have all the time just came forward really fast. There was this scary dark shadow that was touching me and telling me that I should just stop pushing his hands away because this was what married women had to do and that I was going to have to grow up and be married."

Stormy explains, "At the time, I didn't even know what married was. I think I was about three or four years old. I wouldn't do what I was told because he wanted me to perform fellatio on him. He held me down, and I don't remember exactly what happened. I just remember the feelings of pressure on my body and pressure at my vagina. And it hurt really bad. I do remember crying then, and apparently, this went on for quite a while off and on through my younger years."

When Stormy, as a little girl, tried to stand up to her father, he told her that he would get her younger sister to take care of him. "Then I was really confused by the feelings I was having, because I felt that I wasn't good enough and that my sister was better than I was," she says.

Besides the sexual abuse, her father beat the children. He hit them until they had bruises from their shoulders all the way down to the back of their legs. "He was very proud that he only spanked us with a belt on our butts, but he would get mad during those spankings, and still I would have huge bruises all over from the belt," she says.

Stormy says that she carried a lot of shame about the abuse. She felt she was the "naughty little girl" her father told her she was, and that's why he hit her. She lied to her father to try to get him not to hit her. She'd tell him anything she could think of to try to prevent the beatings, but the lying only made her feel worse about herself. As she became old enough to understand what had happened during the sexual abuse, Stormy felt shame about that as well, especially shame that her sister had experienced the same abuse. She felt responsible for her sister's experience.

As a child, Stormy told her friends that her daddy was a great father, and she continued to think of herself as the bad person. Her father told her it was her own fault that she was being beaten, and as any terrified child might, Stormy believed him and became a victim. She could have rebelled, but it was not in her personality. She became subservient to her father to keep the peace. This was especially true after the death of her mother when Stormy was just eleven years old. "My mother was very submissive to my dad because he was so loud and aggressive," Stormy remembers.

One of the effects of this trauma for Stormy is that she struggles with her short-term memory and still has difficulty recalling facts from her childhood when she is in an RTT session. One of the memories that did come up for her was trying to learn her multiplication tables. "I would have to go and write them a hundred times each and then give my dad the paper, and he would drill me. I wouldn't remember them, so he'd hit me with the book and the belt. He would throw things at me. He was very proud because he never hit me with his fist. It was always an open hand," she says.

"One of the first few times I started screaming at the workshop, it just felt so good because even when I was a little girl getting a spanking, I was told not to scream—even though he's hitting me so hard that I'm getting welts. So I never screamed. I could handle an amazing amount of pain and not scream. And after that process, I thought, 'Okay, this is amazingly scary, but I feel so much better right this minute.' After my turn on the mat, I felt filled with light! And after the end of the first workshop, I felt wonderful, as if the colors around me were brighter, stronger," she says.

Shortly after her initial feelings of relief following that first process, Stormy started to feel awful. This seemed to happen consistently after every process during her first workshop. I explained to her that it's like peeling an onion. It may take some time to move and release the emotional energy that has been stuck; as she moves some energy, other energy might come to the surface.

"My 'happies' were a lot happier, but then, when I would be in a bad space or feel grief, it was super-strong. So my happies were happier, but my sadness was a little deeper. And I honestly believe that's because I was actually truly back in my body feeling the sadness. Now, when I do fall and am in a bad space, I know what to do. I can move the energy by myself," she says.

Stormy continues to attend workshops, and while she admits that the journey has sometimes been difficult, "the rewards are everything." What are those rewards? First and foremost, her shoulder pain is gone, and it was relieved early on during her RTT work. "Doing this work has opened my eyes to help me understand that I'm really not a bad person, that I'm actually a very decent person," she says.

Stormy has learned to stay in the moment and keep her heart open, and she can now speak her truth without her emotions taking over. She no longer blames others for her problems.

"I know what true happiness is," Stormy adds. "I know what true bliss is! Every day in my life, I see or feel something that makes my heart feel like it's going to swell up so big with happiness that others will see it! My chest is all pumped up with pure happiness. Every day. It's amazing. Such a wonderful way to live life! I smile so big that it feels like my face will crack in two. This work gave me my life. I didn't even realize I wasn't living."

Cathy's Story

Cathy, who you first met in chapter 3, had suffered for years with severe ulcers that caused shooting pain through her body and made it difficult for her to eat. "I learned how much pain I had been holding in my body throughout my life," she says. "I was even holding pain for other people. I was a sponge that took the pain of others and sucked it in from all sides. I was old before my time due to my experiences with this. I walked, talked, and thought in a very old sense. I had a very deep sense of bitterness that sometimes overwhelmed me. And sometimes, when no one was looking, I would curl up on the floor and not move from the pain that wracked my body. I have a video of me when I was nineteen years old. I look and move as if I am seventy-five to eighty years old."

Dealing with her stuck emotions in RTT sessions allowed Cathy's body to begin to heal. "As I worked on the anxiety, the ulcers never returned," Cathy says. "It has been twelve years, and I've never had to have those treated again. The shooting pains went away as well. Nobody knows what they were, other than just physical symptoms of extreme stress."

Due to her ulcers, Cathy weighed only 120 pounds even though she is five feet, eight inches tall. Now she weighs 145 pounds, which is a healthier weight for her height and frame.

She says that when she came to White Raven Center, she was mostly sitting around and waiting for death—even though she wasn't aware of that until she began to do RTT. Now she works out and takes good care of her body.

Bee's Story

We told one aspect of Bee's story in chapter 5; another facet is that she finds that RTT regularly alleviates physical symptoms. "I can come in and be down and depressed and beating myself up, and my stomach's in knots or I have diarrhea. And I can do a process and feel 100 percent better when I get out," she says.

"I've come down with headaches that are just killing me, and we work through it, and the headache's gone. I had shoulder surgery five years ago—a lot of pain pills and a lot of pain. I came to a workshop, and my prayer for the workshop was that I would get off the pain pills. I wanted the pain to stop," she says. "Saturday afternoon of the workshop, I lay down at White Raven because I wasn't feeling well. My body was hurting, and I felt sick. I couldn't come back upstairs for the rest of the workshop, so everybody came downstairs and touched me with healing energy. Floyd and Marianne said some prayers for me. The next morning, Sunday, my shoulder didn't hurt. I had been taking six pain pills a day, and I was down to one after that."

Jan's Story

Our client Jan, whom you met in chapter 5, also experienced a difference in physical symptoms as a result of RTT processing. "My old self-image included wasted, useless legs," she says. "My body reflected this, as well as the emotions stored from a bad leg injury, with a bad knee that would buckle at unexpected moments and was never quite 'right.' Now my self-image has healthy, normal legs, and my body reflects that with healthy legs that no longer buckle or feel 'off.' If you believe the doctors, the only thing that could have fixed my bum knee was surgery. And they were right to a degree. It took major energetic and emotional surgery, requiring the courage to enter the unknown, to leap into stored terror, and emerge on the other side. But the only surgeon affecting this positive change was me, with the experienced guidance and facilitation of Floyd, Marianne, and their helpers at the White Raven Center."

Kyle's Story

Kyle had a dramatic experience with RTT that quickly resolved several physical issues. "Marianne told me that we have locked up energy that sits in our bodies. Some of that energy can be good, but some can be blocking us from living happy lives," Kyle says. "For me, my energy was preventing me from truly having a bond with people, and that same energy was also causing me lots of health issues. I couldn't sleep through the night, my hands would go numb, I was gaining an incredible amount of weight, I cried all the time, and I was unhappy overall."

As soon as Kyle began the breathing for her first RTT session, her stomach started to tighten. Then she felt as though someone were choking her—a feeling she had experienced before. This was followed by a sensation of her arms and hands tightening.

"The whole time, Marianne was walking me through everything. I never felt scared," Kyle says. "I just couldn't stop the energy from moving. Marianne instructed me to grab hold of a stick and open my mouth to release the energy. I screamed and kicked to get the energy out. The energy flew out of my body so hard and so fast that it knocked things off the high shelves in Marianne's office. Not just once but twice! At first, I thought Marianne had hit something to jar the energy out. It wasn't until I sat up that I realized what had truly happened. Artifacts and candles that had been sitting on the shelves for years had been forced off the shelves, and glass was broken all over the floor. It was really amazing to see. I was tired, but felt calm."

Kyle says she slept like a baby that night and has slept well every night since, which, as of this writing, has been four months.

"For years I had been seeing all kinds of doctors, and nothing worked," Kyle says. "I was getting ready to head to Seattle to see a doctor about my thyroid. Marianne strongly encouraged me to come see her first. She was concerned all the energy I was containing in my body would block anything they tried to do for me. I truly believe she was right! I have seen plenty of doctors before this one with no results. But this time, everything fell into place. My thyroid medication is working, I don't cry anymore, and I feel truly happy. I'm even losing weight! I can't say one session of Rapid Transformation Therapy is all anyone needs, nor can I say that for myself. I may need Marianne's help again, but she has taught me so much in that one session that I will go to her the minute I feel 'off.' My experience with RTT was not only an incredible journey; it was a life-changing event."

Angela's Story

Angela is a counselor who had done quite a bit of traditional therapy. However, she felt that it was difficult to fundamentally change at a core level from engaging solely in talk therapy. Angela's spouse had been working with us for a couple of months. "I was seeing my husband rapidly transform and not really have to go back and grapple with the same issues. There may have been more layers to it, but there was something that was fundamentally different after he got to the core of an issue. The only time I had experienced that to some degree was through non-verbal therapy, which had some similarities but was much more clinical. It didn't go quite as deep [as RTT]." Angela wanted to heal herself emotionally and spiritually so that she could keep her heart more open and have the capacity to love and be loved, to be mindful and present and in her body.

During her first RTT session, Angela experienced what she terms "from the bottom of my soul kind of screaming" into a pillow. Emotions that she didn't even know were inside of her began to emerge. During a workshop, she had a profound experience of communion with her husband. "Essentially, it felt like the first time that my husband and I really joined in our spirits. It felt like we were getting married and what marriage is supposed to be like. I had no idea that was going to happen. It was really powerful. We still struggled after that, but there was something so core that changed that has been different ever since. Things started changing in such powerful ways."

Around that time, Angela and her husband had been trying to conceive a child for six years. Then an opportunity to adopt a baby came their way, and they ceased all efforts to conceive their own biological child. "I really attribute that to my husband and I healing and the work that we've done with White Raven," Angela says. "They didn't give us the baby, but they facilitated and supported our healing in a way that helped us get in alignment with this prayer that we'd been putting out to the universe for years. And it happened."

Then Angela had quite a healing experience during an RTT session. "I literally felt energy shooting out of my reproductive system, out my vagina," she says. "I could feel it, and it felt like everything was opening up and being flushed. I was never one

Physical Symptoms Shift and Heal

to have strong physical sensations like 'Oh, there's a foreign energy form here in my body or I feel this big pain when you pull on that piece of energy from my stomach.' My husband's like that, but I wasn't like that." In this case, it was a very distinct feeling for Angela.

Then, a few months after they adopted their baby, Angela became pregnant. Before RTT she had done hands-on healing work, traditional therapy, homeopathy, acupuncture and other modalities, and she certainly believes these helped the conception along. "But the thing that I think really made a huge difference— and I could feel it energetically—was that flushing out of my reproductive system energetically," she says.

Angela enjoyed a normal pregnancy and gave birth to a healthy baby. The birth experience, however, was a bit traumatic, and she experienced some PTSD from that event. She was surprised to discover that one phone session with Floyd got rid of pretty much all of her symptoms. "People will go to therapy for a long time to heal PTSD!" she says.

Since that experience, Angela has also discovered that many women have PTSD as a result of their birth experiences, and frequently no one talks about it or tries to heal it. She's grateful that she had an opportunity to heal from the birthing trauma so that she can be a better parent.

Rebecca's Story

I remember the evening Rebecca first came to White Raven Center to attend one of our weekend sessions. I answered the door, and Rebecca stood before me holding a small overnight bag in one hand and a CPAP machine in the other. Her energy felt intense, and the first words out of her mouth as she held up her breathing machine were, "Where can I plug in?"

I had previously met Rebecca at the University of Alaska, Anchorage, as she was a student of mine in the bachelor of social work program. At the time, she ran from the opportunity I gave all of my students to participate in a group session at the White Raven Center. Approximately three years after Rebecca graduated, she contacted me to inquire about our services.

Rebecca's initial experiences with RTT took her back to a number of different traumatic events in her life, including the suicide of her boyfriend at age seventeen. "Holy moly, I didn't realize how much trauma I had still been carrying," Rebecca says. "I just let myself really mourn, and then I let him go. It was so powerful. I had also experienced quite a bit of depression. I didn't realize how much until I got to White Raven and had to verbalize and write down how I had been suicidal for a really, really long time. The thoughts were always there. I mean daily. I just never did anything about it."

Rebecca experienced judgment and criticism from family and peers about her weight as a young child. Self-hate festered within Rebecca as a result and, by high school, it manifested in self-destructive behaviors. "I would often drink before school and during school," she says. "I would keep orange juice and vodka in my locker. When I started driving, I even had a little Baileys in my coffee on my way to school. I smoked a lot of pot and did a lot of acid and cocaine. Yeah, I spent a lot of time just being out of my body."

As Rebecca developed more self-awareness, she noticed that she became violently triggered when someone complimented her. "I would want to yell at somebody and lash out if they complimented me," she says. "I also had this one memory that would pop up pretty consistently about when I went to camp when I was eight years old. I had this memory of looking in the mirror before an activity of the day, and I have this really bad boy haircut that I can't believe anyone let me get. But at eight years old, I'm combing my hair, getting ready for the day's activity, and I remember thinking I looked really pretty.

Physical Symptoms Shift and Heal

Then, I remembered there was this certain counselor who was going to be there. I kept looking in the mirror, and my thought was that I don't want to look pretty for him. I reached up and tousled my hair to not make it as feathery and fancy. That's the only memory I ever had. I didn't connect that with anything."

It wasn't long after she started RTT processing that more memories from camp began to surface. I encouraged Rebecca to stay with the memory and look in the mirror. She saw her counselor sitting on a rock down by the lake at camp, and I asked her to go to him in her imagination. She fought the memories. "My mind said nope, that did not happen. I don't remember that. That did not happen," Rebecca says.

When she mustered the courage to walk over to him in her mind's eye, he said, "Rebecca, you look really nice." Her body jumped, and she covered her ears, yelling, "Shut up! Shut up! Shut up!" She tried to insist that she was making it up. She wouldn't believe it.

So, I said, "Okay, but notice what your body is doing. Your body doesn't lie." Rebecca was then able to remember the sexual abuse that she had endured at the age of eight.

"I've believed the lie all this time of this abuser who said no one's going to love you like this," she says. After processing this experience, she is no longer triggered when someone compliments her.

Rebecca's RTT work around being molested by her camp counselor also resolved physical symptoms. "I had this spot on my back in my left shoulder blade area that was just chronic," Rebecca explains. "It just would never ease up. I could maybe get a massage, chiropractic, try to address it. It just never quite resolved. Through this processing, I'd pay attention to body pains that came up in the sessions. It was really clear. I had been on the rocks in the woods for some of this abuse, lying on my back. Then that chronic issue cleared. It was just fascinating that my body was holding on to that physical memory." Rebecca participated in multiple processes around this issue before the pain completely dissolved.

When Rebecca came to us, she was also suffering from chronic jaw pain. "I would have to open my jaw really wide every so often, several times a day. I'd just have to stretch it out, and I'd do it all the time. It was like my jaw was tight," she says. After processing with RTT for a period of time, speaking truth and even raging at her perpetrators, Rebecca's jaw issue resolved.

Another physical symptom that went away after about one and a half years of RTT processing was sleep apnea. "I had what they called 121 brain arousals per hour," she says. "So I was waking up twice a minute. It was pretty severe." Rebecca no longer needs to use her sleep apnea machine. In fact, she gave it away!

As a survival tool, Rebecca had developed an obsessive-compulsive behavior of counting, which she used as a way of staying out of her body and preventing feelings. "I would listen to people speak, and I would count the letters in the words. I would write it with my finger. If somebody said the word 'sound,' I would count how many little finger strokes it took me to write the word. I would actually do it externally until somebody caught me doing it," she says.

"I would count people's facial features when I was speaking to them. It would look like I was engaged, but I was really counting their eyebrows, their eyeballs, their ears, their nose, their nostrils, their lips, their teeth, their tongue. When I started driving, I would add up license plates. It was like heaven. There were letters all over the place. Then I'd add up the numbers and again do how many strokes it took to write the letter or the number. You could count anything," she says.

After the first RTT workshop, Rebecca noticed she didn't count for about twenty-four hours. When she started again the next day, she caught herself in the act and knew that she was trying to avoid feeling. So she asked herself what she had just been thinking. Whenever a group facilitator asks everyone in the group to count, Rebecca says, "I'm not counting. It's like handing me a joint." This was one of Rebecca's primary numbing techniques prior to participating in RTT work. Now she's aware of the behavior and can stay in her body and stay with the feelings, rather than escape into her habitual counting behavior.

Several years into her work, I could see that Rebecca had great potential to be a gifted RTT facilitator. One day, I made a suggestion that encouraged her in this direction. At first, Rebecca questioned her own ability to offer the service of holding space for others' healing. Eventually, she warmed to the idea and allowed herself to naturally evolve into becoming one of our full-time RTT facilitators. "The peace and contentment that I experience now would have been unfathomable to me years ago," she says. "I'm still a human, and I still experience triggers. But I am always grateful when there's a part of myself that is activated or triggered and there's more healing."

Rebecca also transformed years of rescuing and caretaking through processing with RTT. "I now feel absolutely no need to rescue people, no need to fix anybody else, no need to protect people from their own pain or their own problems," she says.

Healing the Physical Through Emotional Release

The stories I have shared in this chapter are a small sample of the types of physical shifts and healings that we witness as a result of the RTT process. We have witnessed physical healing on many levels, including sleep apnea, fibromyalgia, cancer, eating disorders, TMJ or lockjaw, lower back and shoulder pain, chronic headaches and, as in Angela's case, the ability to conceive a child. There are, of course, many variables in an individual's life journey that may contribute to the overall healing outcome. Some of these include attitude, nutritional health, exercise, change of environment, support groups, acupuncture, massage, and the list goes on.

While we have conducted no scientific clinical studies, the anecdotal data and clinical observation from eighteen years of practice with the RTT methodology substantiates a profound correlation between this method and clients' physical healing.

"Everything is energy,
and that's all there is to it.
Match the frequency
of the reality
you want,
and you cannot help
but get that reality.
It can be no other way.
This is not philosophy.
This is physics."

—Darryl Anka

Chapter 9

Understanding and Clearing Energy Attachments

Eventually, the repressed pain in our bodies can become so great that it becomes like an independent energy form—an entity that wants to survive. It uses the electric charge of the repressed pain to maintain control and to keep us in a state of confusion, to keep us doubting ourselves. This entity is like a magnet and draws to us other beings with a matching charge. This escalates the pain in the body as it downloads volumes of energy. It is like the entity is on a feeding frenzy.

We have a tendency to run away from this electrical charge; we deny it and pretend it doesn't exist. One way it possesses us is when it turns into an addiction. We can continue to deny it, or we can face it with human witness. If we choose to face this electrical charge, the power of the entity diminishes. We can then stand and look in the mirror and realize we have been punishing ourselves. We awaken to the fact that we anchored core beliefs from the ones who taught us because they truly believed those beliefs themselves. This is one of the places in RTT where we may have an "Aha!" moment, when we discover that we are our own teacher. As we realize this, the body automatically enters a state of calm.

As each one of us allows for core emotional energy to be released, we awaken within us the brilliance of our own light, and this frees other energy forms that have been contained in our bodies.

Understanding and Clearing Energy Attachments

We all vibrate at a certain frequency, and we attract to us other beings and energy forms that vibrate at a matching frequency. When our bodies contain heavy energies that are connected to our repressed emotions, such as fear, anger, rage, low self-worth, grief, hate, shame, guilt and jealousy, the natural law of attraction dictates that we attract other low vibrational energies. This is completely unconscious. As these unseen energies accumulate in the body, they increasingly confuse our thought processes and pull us away from our heart's desire and what we deserve. Depending on the nature and extent of our traumatic life experience, these energy attachments will control and dictate to varying degrees what happens in our lives. They can become like powerful magnets, attracting things we do not want and keeping us trapped in unhealthy and unproductive cycles.

When we move the heavy, stored core emotional energies, everything in the body's energetic system shifts and changes. As a result, the energy forms that were feeding on our negativity lose their connection to us. We feel lighter, like we have more space inside.

How do these energy forms come to us in the first place? While there are numerous ways this can happen, some of the primary ways include: when a baby or small child is abandoned or neglected, the experience of terror opens them up and they become vulnerable; we also become vulnerable when spending a lot of time as a hospital patient, when we are sedated, when we engage in heavy drug/alcohol use, or when our primary focus is on negative thought patterns and beliefs. Sometimes, these energy forms interfere with our experience by intensifying our emotional reactions, causing confusion and physical pain.

On Saturday evenings at our weekend workshops, we routinely set aside time for clearing of these energy attachments. We spend some time talking about the concept of energy attachments or energy forms, and how they may not be serving our highest good. Then the facilitators work with each client to move attachments from their energy field. This is a type of energy healing process, and attachments are also routinely moved as a natural part of RTT processing.

For example, Toby recently worked with a new client who had never heard of an energy attachment. He perceived that she had one, so he worked with her to release it during her RTT session. The woman began to sob, and Toby instructed her to say, "This is MY body! Nothing belongs in this body but me. Leave now!" Then, abruptly, the emotion stopped, and the client said, "Is it possible that I could have been feeling something that wasn't me?" She felt that the emotion she experienced really had nothing to do with her. Toby then explained to her that he had indeed felt that there was an energy attachment in her energy field.[10] Such attachments can manifest as emotions that really aren't based in your own experience. This was her raw experience, with no preconceived ideas about it.

When we perceive an energy attachment in someone's field as Toby did, it's an intuitive knowing and awareness. Our client Arlene puts it this way: "I say to people, 'Can you remember back to a time when you were little, and you walked into a room and knew something was wrong but didn't know why? You could tell, without asking any questions, that people had been fighting before you walked in.' When I ask them how they knew that, they answer, 'Because I could feel it.' But when I press them about how they could feel it, they say they don't know, but they insist they could just feel it and know that the people in the room had been fighting." This is not unlike what we experience when we perceive energetic forms during our work.

At times, we perceive an energy attachment in someone's energy field and discover that the individual has been

---

[10] The human energy field is also sometimes called the aura. We understand that this field of energy can collect energies from outside of us, and that emo- tional disturbances that start in the energy field may eventually, if not healed, become physical ailments.

experiencing body pain near that area. Once the attachment has been removed, the client normally reports a shift in their level of pain.

Arlene's Story

Arlene, who you first met in chapter 5, experienced an energy attachment after giving birth to her second son. He was in the hospital, and she had to spend a lot of time there. She was diagnosed as having postpartum depression and suicidal ideation. Six months later, she recalls sitting at the dinner table and hearing a voice in her head say, "You should just kill yourself. You won't hurt anymore." She says these kinds of thoughts continued for about four months, but they weren't the same as insecurities or negative feelings she had felt in the past.

When she finally told someone at White Raven Center about what she was experiencing and came in for a process, the facilitator was able to help Arlene clear an energy form that seemed to be connected to the voice she was hearing. "I felt better instantly," Arlene says. "I was able to sleep again. There was nothing dramatic about the process. It was simply a matter of telling the energy to leave, and the voice stopped."

Because Arlene had completed many deep core emotional healing sessions, this energy form was exposed—instead of hidden deep in her energy field, which can be the case for those who hold much repressed emotional energy—and could be released with ease. This is a good example to remind us that the negative voice in our minds is not who we are, whether it is an energy attachment or the voice of a negative adult from childhood.

Angela's Story

During a telephone session with Floyd, Angela asked, "Do I have to go in through the victim?"

"Spirit knows," Floyd responded, meaning that her higher self, as well as any angels or helpful spirits around her, would know what she needed to do in order to heal.

Angela had been "processing" her emotions on her own in various ways, but she hadn't learned how to go into her emotions and feel her pain without assuming the role of "the victim." What she was referring to was going into the core—the inner place where we most deeply suppress our pain. She felt anxiety and anger, which manifested as an ache in her sternum. Angela was aware that this energy had become stuck. She felt powerless and could cry tears of grief, but she also felt her spirit leading her toward an inner strength that was preparing to emerge.

At that time, the main trigger in Angela's life was her adopted two-year-old daughter. Angela sometimes felt what she described as extreme anger toward her daughter, and she wrestled with tremendous guilt because of it. The only way she knew how to handle the situation was to suppress the anger and close her heart. "Leading up to the appointment time with Floyd, I got increasingly triggered by my daughter. I was angry at her all the time, wanting to yell at her," Angela described.

When Floyd led Angela into her emotions through the breath, she immediately sensed a presence inside of her that was resisting her attempt at feeling, breathing, and speaking her truth. Floyd then asked her, "Who are you angry at?" When Angela yelled her daughter's name, Floyd said, "Just tell her."

"It was a feeling of wanting to lash out and scream and hit and kick and all sorts of stuff—more of a physical experience," Angela says. "I needed to punch and hit and kick. I grabbed a pillow and did a growl like an aggressive scream."

As Angela sat up and beat the pillow forcefully, Floyd attempted to move her to a place where she could speak her truth with the knowledge that she wasn't really going to hurt her daughter in any way. The victim in her had never been able to claim her truth; only her weakness. "It's not really your daughter you're hitting or yelling at," he said gently to Angela.

With that, Angela was able to express her truth without apology. "You stupid little brat! I hate you! You make everything hard! Get out of my life!" she shouted.

The little girl had come to represent the pain that Angela had been carrying since she was a child of the same age. Much like Mitch and Renee in previous chapters, that trauma was triggered when her daughter reached the same age. When Angela was two years old, her rambunctious nature had angered her father intensely; his reactions frightened Angela, traumatizing her.

In this case an entity attachment was activated, and that entity's voice emerged as Angela spoke—an entity that had been masquerading as her daughter. The entity was attached to Angela, and it created an illusion that her anger with her daughter was real. In reality, though, her daughter was simply triggering the intense, repressed anger that Angela held toward her own father. The image of her daughter was really just a mirror of her own hurt inner child.

After Angela had kicked and screamed and expressed her anger until she collapsed, Floyd suggested, "See your daughter in front of you." In her mind's eye, Angela looked into her daughter's eyes. They turned black, and the entity emerged. It was exposed, unable to hide behind the innocent face of the child any longer. Floyd began to move the entity out with the various energy healing tools he has come to know and practice. Angela participated fully in the process by visualizing herself being cleansed by a brilliant white light. To close the session, Floyd had Angela connect once again with her daughter's eyes.

Rapid Transformation Therapy

This time, there was no emotional trigger, and love and light flowed between the two.

As you can see, these energy attachment experiences can run the gamut during RTT. It's important to approach whatever comes forward in a session with an open mind, and to know that moving the stored core emotional energy is central to the entire healing process. Clients do participate in the clearing process and, no matter how intense the energy form may be, the key to healing is always with the willingness and intent of the client.

"To know yourself as the being
underneath the thinker,
the stillness underneath the mental noise,
the love and joy underneath the pain,
is freedom, salvation, enlightenment."

—Eckhart Tolle

Chapter 10

Maintaining a Transformed State of Inner Peace

Our friend, Larry, came running into our office one day because he felt so much better after taking a stick and raging on a tree. The following day, he shared that he had "replenished" his rage and was experiencing extreme frustration. His experience illustrates how we can go out in the woods and scream our bloody heads off and experience temporary relief—but if we don't have a human witness and make conscious shifts with regard to our experience, we are likely to draw the same energy back to us and recycle it later.

It is true that it can take multiple processes to transform all of the energy connected to one traumatic event. This is because some experiences are so intense that the volume of energy can only be felt and moved in increments. For example, if you're an infant who is repeatedly left alone in your crib without routine care, the energy of terror from that experience is so locked into your body that it can take a number of sessions to release all the stored energy safely. As a result, it may be difficult to discern whether you are recycling energy or simply moving through the next stage of stored energy for the first time.

Recycling primarily occurs when we remain isolated, not sharing our truth with others, and when we don't change the self-destructive behaviors and patterns that keep us trapped in a cycle of suffering. For example, I had one client who did numerous RTT sessions with us but kept her addiction to purging a secret. It became clear that she was recycling energy as she continued her self-destructive behavior. Once she spoke the truth about her addiction, she eliminated the need to recycle the energy of shame that had been connected to her behavior.

When we allow our anger to be fully present and express it without judgment, we break the pattern of recycling. This also holds true when we come out of silence and express deep inner truth. The result is that we move out of the role of victim and take responsibility for ourselves. It's important to point out, however, that taking responsibility is not the same as inflicting blame on ourselves. Self-blame keeps us in the victim position, while responsibility empowers us and allows us to take charge of our lives and move forward. Self-blame is a place of defeat, while responsibility means we hold the power of change.

My client who revealed her addiction to purging disclosed many layers of guilt and shame connected to her body image. During that session she used those memories to go deeper into her repressed feelings and give them back to the source, which was her abusive mother. She unplugged the shame, unloaded her feelings of anger and blame, and eventually came to forgive her mother, who was reacting out of her own repressed pain. Now she feels empowered to nurture her own soul.

Much of the pain we feel in our lives is the result of the stories we tell ourselves about the events of our lives—the beliefs we have come to think of as truth. For instance, if I have stored emotional energy from believing I'm not good enough, I will have to repeatedly release that emotional energy until I actually change the inner voice that says, "I am not good enough." When we become aware of these beliefs and the punitive language we repeatedly use against ourselves, we can take responsibility for creating them and "catch ourselves in the act" of reiterating self-damaging beliefs.

We might catch ourselves in the midst of self-judgment, for example. Rather than judge the judgment—a double whammy— we learn to simply observe: "Oh, I just judged myself." Noticing and immediately releasing the blame are half the challenge. As soon as we observe and acknowledge the judgment, we are present in the moment and outside of the drama. Then we have the opportunity to change the self-limiting beliefs we have told ourselves.

Maintenance and Self-Care

Once we have shifted the energy from within and experienced a sense of calm, we want to maintain that shift. We don't want to recycle the energy we worked so hard to release. But how do we do it? There are numerous practices that can contribute to sustaining a sense of inner calm.

One important maintenance practice is to keep the energy moving. When we first dive into RTT processing, it's similar to opening a floodgate. The energy wants to keep moving, and the universe will provide every opportunity for this to happen. We do not want to revert to blocking the energy again. This requires us to continue sharing simple truth in the moment with our fellow human beings—with words and with our feelings—so that emotional energy does not get stuck.

Bear in mind that the ego wants us to keep suffering by closing our hearts and falling back into old, self-destructive patterns. The ego is not actively or consciously malicious; its nature simply resonates with the human tendency to identify our source of well- being as existing someplace outside the self. In fact, sustainable well-being comes from within, and can only be achieved with an open heart. This is one reason it's so critical to reach out for human support and witness as you work through your feelings. If you feel deep energies activated within you, or if you feel extremely emotional and scared, it may be time to arrange for a healing session in order to move that energy.

Maintaining a Transformed State of Inner Peace

Speaking truth is a critical piece of the maintenance puzzle. As I have said, there is incredible value in sharing truth with another human being. We accept the value of all other healing modalities, including talk therapy, and we encourage you to do the same. Speaking truth in talk therapy is an excellent way to achieve greater awareness and maintain the peace and calm experienced through RTT. When individuals elect to move beyond talk therapy and engage in a deeper healing modality such as RTT, it doesn't eliminate the need for (or therapeutic value of) continuing to share truth.

When we start to own our feelings and speak truth consistently, we stop projecting onto others and begin to heal. "Feeling is healing," and feeling at core levels is life-transforming. For example, our client Roberta witnessed constant quarreling between her parents when she was a little girl, each blaming the other for how they felt. As they argued, neither parent even noticed that their child was observing them. Because Roberta loved her parents and wanted them to be happy, she blamed herself for their conflict. As an adult, whenever conflict occurs, Roberta reacts with guilt and defensiveness because she unconsciously believes it's her fault.

As part of her recovery, Roberta practices speaking truth to her husband whenever there's conflict between them. She might say, "When you express anger, it triggers childhood memories of my parents arguing." This dialogue defuses the intensity of the emotions in the moment. Her husband begins to understand why Roberta overreacts during arguments, which helps him shift his energy of anger to understanding and compassion. Roberta's support system now includes her husband.

As we continue to move the energy of stored emotions, we open up the space to become aware of the self-limiting beliefs we've been telling ourselves. We become non-judgmental observers or witnesses, bringing consciousness to the attitudes, behaviors, and thoughts that have contributed to our pain. Eventually we learn how to resist the seduction of self-doubt, as we become mindful and make a commitment to becoming impeccable with our words and thoughts.

Below are some other powerful ways to maintain the transformed state:

Break the cycle of isolation. Many clients have a habit of isolating themselves so they can hide their emotions and avoid being hurt. This, however, just puts the inner wounded child in the driver's seat. Some people break out of their isolation by enrolling in art classes, quilting classes, yoga, and the like. Social activities help us break through the habit of isolating ourselves.

In one of her sessions, Tia spoke a powerful truth with regard to isolation. She flung off her blindfold and blurted out, "I need to look you in the eyes! I am tired of living like this. I'm tired of the shame, I'm tired of the secrets, and I'm tired of hiding. I want to walk the circle and look others in the eyes. I'm sick of keeping my blinds closed, even during the day, and I have had it with being afraid every night." Tia is now stepping out in the community by volunteering to help children in need.

Create a support community. Each participant in our White Raven Center healing weekends leaves with a contact list. We encourage clients to stay in contact with the individuals they have formed a connection with over the weekend. Beyond the connections made through White Raven, we encourage participants to find a community that will support them on their healing journey. As we become more in balance with ourselves, we attract like-minded souls into our community support group.

Reading to nurture your soul. As part of maintenance work, I encourage people to read. Walk into a bookstore and allow yourself to be drawn to just the right book for you. Pick up several books from the self-help and spirituality sections and read a bit of each. See what resonates with your soul or what words call to you. If you don't like to read, get the audiobook. Please see our short list of recommended reading in Appendix D.

> "We must go beyond the constant clamor of
> ego, beyond the tools of logic and reason,
> to the still, calm place within us: the realm of the soul."
>
> —Deepak Chopra

Meditation. There are so many forms of meditation, and you can choose whichever one you like. Meditation doesn't necessarily mean sitting still and quiet. You can meditate while practicing yoga, gardening, walking, cleaning, swimming, and many other tranquil activities. There is no right or wrong way, yet practicing some form of meditation can help you maintain the transformation from your suffering. That said, starting with a group practice is a powerful way for beginners to learn how to meditate.

Experiment in order to find the meditation technique or combination of techniques that work best for you. If you have never meditated, it's like the calm feeling you experience as you drift off to sleep. The intent of meditation is to connect with what I call the universal mind, where deeper insights are revealed to us. In our society, we have all been programmed to believe that the voice of the chattering ego mind is who we are. Nothing could be further from the truth. Identification with the mind chatter can make you feel panicky, maybe even as if you're going crazy at times. This generates fear, which moves us out and away from our bodies.

When you meditate, you anchor yourself in your body center and relinquish the obsessive nature of the conscious mind, which continually tries to figure out past experiences or how to avoid pain in the future. That obsession contributes to obsessive/ compulsive behavior and results in recycling of your energy, instead of consciously choosing how and where to direct it.

The conscious ego mind does not want to relinquish control. The ego mind wants perfection. It habitually finds fault and looks for more, more, more. In the meditative state you surrender to what is true in the moment, even though you may observe the many directions the conscious mind is trying to pull you. The universal mind accepts what is and knows it is perfect. When you meditate, you give yourself the gift of knowing and feeling your divine perfection.

Cleansing activities. Nourishing self-care activities like taking steam baths, hot baths, and participating in sweat lodges can cleanse your energetic and physical systems and relax you, drawing you more fully into the present moment. You may want to add a cup of sea salt to your hot bath, or eucalyptus to your steam bath, for further relaxation and cleansing.

Exercise and nutrition. When we are emotionally disconnected and out of the body, we tend to be irritable, anxious, frustrated and even angry. We normally don't recognize the symptoms of nutritional imbalance, dehydration, lack of exercise, low blood sugar and exhaustion. Once we bring consciousness (our soul parts) back into our bodies, we come to realize that the body has its own language. As we tune in we become able to hear the body's call for rest, nourishment, and exercise. Listening to and acting on the wisdom your body provides will make a significant contribution to maintaining your healing and balance—both physical and emotional.

Intuition. When we close our hearts, leave our bodies and disconnect from our own presence, we cut ourselves off from our inner guidance. We do this unconsciously and without the recognition that we are literally cutting off our lifeline to the most powerful source of wisdom in the universe.

We all have an internal guide. I call it my inner pendulum. It's generally referred to as intuition. This is the place God communicates with us—the place where, when we tune in and listen, we receive guidance that will never steer us wrong. Learning to connect with and use your intuition takes practice. Yet it is one of the most valuable tools you have for self-awareness and life direction.

Self-observation. In order to maintain the shifts we make through RTT, we must become observers of ourselves and others. We watch ourselves begin to feel triggered, and start to catch ourselves before we overreact emotionally. We notice how we feel in certain circumstances and determine why those feelings are present. For example, a man might notice that he wants to lash out at his wife because she has said something that reminded him of his abusive father. Rather than re-inflict the pain on his wife by yelling at her, he pauses and uses the self-observation skills that have evolved from doing his deep inner work. Then he shares truth with his wife: "I'm feeling really angry, and I want to blame you. I see that you are triggering unresolved feelings I have toward my father. I don't want to take my anger out on you." In this situation, if the wife is in a centered place and also doing her RTT work, her husband may ask her to be his witness, to "hold space" while he moves stored emotional energy in a safe manner. Or he may choose to explore that trigger during his next emotional processing session.

As we become better observers of self, we come to understand that there is a reciprocal relationship between our inner and outer worlds. What happens inside of us manifests around us. Everything before us is a mirror. When we constantly blame the outside world for our situation or look to others to fill us with the love and acceptance we feel we lack, it's a clear signal that it's time to look within. Similarly, the more aware we become, the more we are able to manifest what we desire in life from a place of conscious choice.

Self-observation also helps heal habitual caretaking behaviors. We begin to observe how we react to the pain and suffering of others, recognizing that we have a choice in all situations. We can choose to act with compassion or encouragement, or we can continue to react and engage in mutual suffering. In our society, it's common to show love by hurting with others who are in pain. For example, couples commonly take on each other's pain during times of great challenge and suffering. The goal is to learn to observe without taking on the pain of others. It's possible to keep our hearts open to ourselves, and to others, without an emotional reaction.

Daily self-observation practice involves saying to the ego mind, "I see you, and I refuse to take the path of suffering. In this moment, I choose the path of love." This practice will contribute significantly to sustaining your transformation.

Breathing. In order to maintain the shifts that occur during RTT processing sessions, we must practice staying present in the moment. One way to do this is by paying attention to our breath. If you notice that your breathing is shallow, you are starving your brain of oxygen and perpetuating a feeling of numbness. You will likely feel sluggish, unmotivated, and cut off from your feelings. This is almost always an unconscious pattern from childhood that your body relapses into.

Notice that when you breathe deeply, you become more energized, more alive, and more awake on every level. You will feel more—the whole gamut of feelings, from highs to lows. If you're struggling to stay present, focus on your breath and notice what is going on in your body. "What do my toes feel like right now? What do my fingers feel like right now?" It's a simple method to bring you back into your body and the sensations of now.

Anchoring Soul Parts

When soul retrieval has occurred, it's a wonderful feeling to welcome back a part of the self that might have been lost many years ago. People report feeling more whole, more peaceful, and sometimes even a greater capacity to express all sorts of feelings. It isn't uncommon, however, for the soul part that has been retrieved to go back into hiding. This happens especially if we continue negative self-talk or behaviors that caused the soul part to hide in the first place. Therefore, holding onto soul parts is a powerful aspect of maintenance practice. We call this maintenance process "anchoring."

Our client Bee was so emotionally and mentally battered by her now-deceased mother that even after many soul parts returned, the voice of her mother remained in her mind, continuing the cycle of victimization and damage to the soul. Bee was totally convinced that she was ugly, stupid, worthless and undeserving of love. Her self-talk consisted of her mother's voice in her head, relentlessly putting her down at every turn. As a result, many of the soul parts that Bee had retrieved during RTT went back into hiding. They couldn't bear to feel the abuse again.

Eventually Bee realized that she was recycling her childhood trauma and, over time, she learned to stop screaming at her own inner little girl in the same way as her mother. It took repeated participatory soul retrieval journeys and maintenance work to release that inner voice she had known for so long. Ultimately, however, she was able to anchor the soul parts that had been lost and nurture them in the way she had always wanted to be nurtured by her own mother.

So, how do you anchor your soul parts? There are as many different ways as there are people. For anchoring to work, however, it's important to allow the soul part to continue to speak his or her truth. We often have a habit of shutting that voice down. Part of anchoring is being aware of when truth needs to be spoken again. This involves staying connected to the newly recovered soul part.

In the soul retrieval chapter, I mentioned how Amy anchored her soul parts by engaging in activities that she had enjoyed when she was younger. Another of our clients, Lilly, had a soul retrieval with a twelve-year-old part of her, and that part wanted chocolate cake. So Lilly went home from her session and made a chocolate cake. Another client's two-year-old soul part asked if the client would take her back to a favorite childhood spot where she had often lifted a rock and watched an ant's nest. The client wasn't able to create this experience in the physical realm, so she used her imagination to enjoy the same result.

Some of our clients have created altars and daily rituals, such as lighting candles every morning, to honor and acknowledge their soul parts. As an example, Toby placed photos of himself at different ages on an altar and sang songs to his little boy selves. Each day, he asked them what they needed. "If they needed softness, I might put a cotton ball on the altar," he says. "Keeping it in the physical helped me to remind myself to honor these parts."

We sometimes suggest to clients that they say the following to their soul parts, either during an RTT processing session or during maintenance: "This is [insert the current year]. This is a new day. All that you shared and expressed did happen, but it isn't happening now. Home is right here in this body, which belongs to you and to me. This is your home, too. I understand now that you are the reason I have felt empty my whole life. I have missed you, and I've never felt complete without you. It's time for you to come home and stay here at home with me."

These rituals demonstrate to your soul parts that it's safe to stay out of hiding. The more compassion, caring, understanding, gentleness and acceptance you show these parts of you, the more likely they will stay anchored within your soul being.

What Is Nurturing to the Soul vs. Damaging to the Soul?

In every moment, we have a choice to nurture or damage our souls. Each one of us has to discern for ourselves what is soul-nurturing and what is soul-damaging. You can ask yourself, "Is this relationship soul-nurturing or soul-damaging to me? Is it prolonging my suffering?" If a relationship or other situation requires that you give your power away, you aren't

Maintaining a Transformed State of Inner Peace

present with yourself. This leaves you vulnerable to damaging your soul.

If another person or situation is the source of your well-being—if you feel you must rely on this person or circumstance outside of yourself in order to be okay—that's an experience of giving your power away. Soul-nurturing involves taking full responsibility for your experience and unconditionally accepting what is . . . right now in this moment.

Some choices surrounding relationships or circumstances can be neutral. In these situations, we have a choice that does not affect the integrity or well-being of our souls. Ultimately, the bottom-line question remains: *Is my heart open to me?*

By maintaining a personal commitment to your ongoing healing process, you discover that you are truly living life as opposed to merely surviving it. As humans, we are meant to be in a perpetual state of calm and inner peace. When we are merely surviving, we focus on the fear. When we open our hearts to the love that lives inside of us and honor all of our experiences as opportunities for learning and healing, we truly embrace and enjoy the life we have been gifted.

(See Appendix C for a version of the White Raven Center Tool Kit, which we offer as support for maintenance and self-care.)

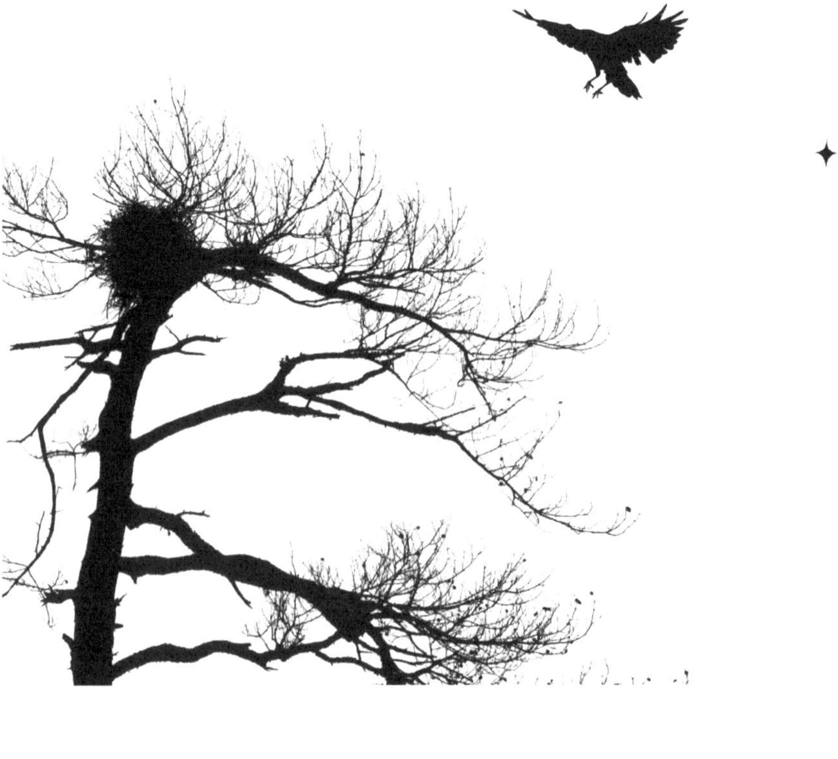

"We cultivate love when we allow
our most vulnerable
and powerful selves to be deeply seen
and known, and when we honor
the spiritual connection
that grows from that offering with trust,
respect, kindness, and affection."

—Brené Brown

Chapter 11

Tips for Practitioners and Individuals Who Want to Try RTT

As helpers, we must sit in full presence with our clients, maintaining an open heart and a clear mind. If you want to serve as an RTT support person, you must be in a calm, secure and centered state of being. You should never attempt to support another's journey during a time when you are struggling or in a triggered state yourself. The client will be able to feel if something is going on with you, and could become overly concerned about your well-being. This could cause the client to repeat dysfunctional patterns of rescuing/caretaking.

Before a session, I always tell my clients to let go of any expectations. It's a good idea to set an intent for the healing you're seeking during the session; after that intent has been set, it is best to let go and take the ride. I invite clients to stay open to the journey that their soul knows they are prepared to take at this particular time.

As helpers, we can't tell another person what they're going to experience or what is going to happen. We must serve as a clean slate, allowing the deepest truth to unfold for the client. When we as helpers are fully present and hold space for another human being with an open heart and no expectations, the healing is mutually beneficial.

Creating Sacred Space

At the White Raven Center, we frequently receive feedback that we have created an environment that is warm, nurturing, welcoming, and safe for our clients. Daniel, whose story you previously read, opened his eyes after one of our sessions and said, "This place is so sacred, Marianne. I just love this place." His comment is far from uncommon. After our workshops, most participants say they wish they could stay because it feels so safe to them.

Creating a sacred space to work in helps clients feel safe enough to enter the deepest and most uncharted territories of their beings. It helps them find the courage to take the terrifying walk from the conscious mind into the heart. It wraps them in a blanket of love that gives true healing a chance to begin.

On the other hand, RTT can be performed anywhere. The most important thing to keep in mind is that the energy we carry as practitioners must be generated from a place of love, respect, and acceptance, and we must stay fully present in our bodies. It is an honor and a privilege to bear witness to another's deepest pain. That, in itself, is sacred.

A Note About Other Participants/Observers

During our workshops at White Raven Center, we continue to do sessions until everyone has worked. This means that we sometimes work into the wee hours, especially on our first night (Friday). We tell our participants that if they feel sleepy or feel the need to leave during someone's process, they can do so quietly.

Everyone is instructed to take care of their own needs, yet remain as present as possible when they choose to stay and observe.

If someone becomes triggered while observing, however, and feels the need to scream and burst out during someone else's process, we encourage them to do it. We don't hold back any feelings during a workshop. If someone feels too ashamed or afraid to let themselves show their emotions, they need to go fully into those feelings of shame or fear.

We also guard against caretaking during RTT sessions. If we soothe someone while in process, we can shut down their feelings. We hug and soothe *after* the process has taken place. During the process, we give each participant the maximum opportunity to stay with the feelings, however painful they may be, in order to move those feelings through.

Preparing for the Session

Reassure the client that no one ever gets hurt in the safe environment that you have created. In addition to maintaining the energy of presence, love, respect and acceptance, you create that safe place by establishing safety guidelines that match the circumstances and physical surroundings available for the session. For example, in Kent's case as previously shared, we elicited support from a dozen other participants to create a wall of padded mats that he could safely attack. If other people are not available to support, we would offer the client an alternative means to release the same repressed energy, i.e., Kent could have been instructed to pull on a pole to create tension as he screamed. The bottom line is that you, as the facilitator, must use discretion and common sense to create a safe environment in which nobody gets hurt.

Once the client either lies down on a mat on the floor or is seated comfortably in a chair, ask if anything else is needed for physical comfort. Adjust the room temperature and blankets according to their needs, and let the client know

Tips for Practitioners and Individuals Who Want to Try RTT

that temperature adjustments, blankets, and pillows can be provided at any point in the process. (Once emotional energy has moved the body normally becomes toasty warm, and the client will likely start tossing off the blankets.) If the person is lying face-up, place a bolster under the knees to ease pain and tension in the back.

Place a blindfold over the client's eyes, explaining that this will allow him/her to journey within and remain focused on the inner experience. Make sure the blindfold shuts out light entirely. We use sleeping masks with an elastic strap, because they are comfortable and easy to adjust.

Review the simple breathing technique with the client, reminding him/her to take a deep, conscious breath and to notice the belly rising as if they are blowing up a balloon. Explain that the purpose of this technique is to quiet the pull of the busy mind and facilitate a deeper connection with core emotions. Client experiences vary. Some have a difficult time breathing from the abdomen and need to relearn what was a natural process as a baby. (This comes from learning to hold the breath to numb feelings.) At times, the facilitator may engage in the breathwork with the client by breathing with them, demonstrating the depth and intensity of the technique. In some cases, when clients are having difficulty moving away from the mind and into core energies, the facilitator may elect to guide the client by using the birthing breath technique of two quick breaths in and one longer, deeper breath out in rapid succession.

Explain that facilitator and client both share the intention to listen to the wisdom of the body and the soul, allowing it to speak to you and guide you both. It is extremely important that the participant understand that his/her body may move, shake, vibrate, or even experience temporary paralysis or gnarling of the hands. Explain that the conscious mind will attempt to define what is happening, and encourage the client to surrender to the experience.

During the Core Emotional Healing Portion of the RTT Session

Ask the client to begin the breathing process by taking deep, slow breaths and filling up the belly. As the client connects with his/her core emotions, your job is to bear witness as they speak or demonstrate truth. If you sense that he or she is retreating from the feelings, encouraging and empowering phrases like "Stay with it," "You are doing beautiful work," and "You're not alone; keep going," may help him/her remember that it's safe to go back into the deep emotions.

Urge the client to keep going as he/she transforms and moves the energy out of the body. This happens naturally as the deep breathing activates pent-up emotional energy, and the supporting, non-judgmental witness of another human being validates the truth of the client's inner experience. If he/she experiences significant physical pain, tension, or purging symptoms,[11] remind him/her that this is only energy moving. Reiterate that the client is in a safe place and that the energy is not who they are.

Stay with the client throughout the process. Periodically check in, asking what he/she is experiencing in the moment—especially when there are long periods of silence.

Encourage the client to continue sharing his/her truth out loud throughout the process.

As clients share their experience during sessions, encourage them to continue to walk through their (figurative) door of truth. For example, if the client sees shadows or figures in the distance, you might ask him/her to take charge by moving closer in spite of feelings of fear.

---

[11] Purging symptoms can come up during RTT, such as coughing up phlegm, releasing excessive nostril mucus, and even vomiting as a means of purging toxins.

It might be helpful at some point for you, or someone else in the room, to play the part of an individual in the client's story. For example, you might remember that Floyd allowed a client to hold his face while the client remained blindfolded, as a representation of the client's father. Another time, a female client was speaking her truth to her father, and another participant in the room served as the voice of her father so that the dialogue could be made more real to her. It's important that the helping participants allow the lead facilitator to guide all aspects of the session. As the professional in the room you will direct the dialogue, telling the other participant what to say so that the client's experience is one of healing and not one of re-traumatization or confusion. It takes time and practice to develop this skill, and practitioners of RTT must have direct experience with the process themselves.

If the client is struggling to get in touch with emotions, continue with the breath, and ask him or her to speak the truth of his/her feelings in the moment. It could simply be, "I don't want to do this. I don't like it here. I hate this." Speaking this truth helps to open the energy. As facilitators, we sometimes offer things for the client to say based on what we know about the client. For example, "Mom, I hate you." This can be difficult to say; sometimes it may feel right to the client, and sometimes not. We ask the client to "try on" our suggestions as a way of opening the door to the deeper core feelings.

Physical Experiences, Assistance, and Tools During RTT

Some of the techniques that follow require years of experience to safely implement. Our primary rule at the White Raven Center is safety. We never want to traumatize another human being when we are actually trying to help them heal from trauma. It is critical that each participant maintain an ongoing dialogue with the lead facilitator. These techniques are intense, so the result can be life-transforming and miraculous when done appropriately and responsibly. Please do not attempt these techniques without training, guidance, and experience.

Our body's natural capacity to heal can be activated during an RTT session, and the body might want to expel stored toxins. As previously mentioned, this can involve purging symptoms.

Clients also sometimes feel different body temperatures at various points in the process. One client began shivering and violently shaking every time he started to process. Even his teeth chattered. He was awakening body memories of a time as a young boy when he had almost frozen to death.

For some clients, a great deal of tension manifests in certain parts of the body during a session. For example, Lilly experienced gnarled hands when she revisited the trauma of her sister nearly drowning her. This was her body's physical expression of how much energy she had blocked in order to survive the intense fear and panic she experienced at the time of her trauma. Another client held so much pain stored in her feet that when we touched certain spots, she screamed in agony as pain shot up through her legs. Remember that these symptoms are just manifestations of the energy moving through the body. As the aforementioned clients continued through their respective RTT processes, the body symptoms diminished and their bodies returned to a state of calm.

The body can also manifest pockets of energy that create pain in the body. Tia, who experienced horrible abuse as a child and whose story you've already heard parts of, had to delve into those deep pockets. Sometimes, she just had to scream for a long time until the pain finally dissolved. "What's weird is that I needed that pain to feel alive," Tia explains. She needed to feel that physical pain in order to trigger the emotions and memories connected to those traumatic life experiences.

Tips for Practitioners and Individuals Who Want to Try RTT

She might say, "Marianne, I'm feeling this really horrible pain in my side. Could you put your fingers there?" With my fingers touching that spot, sometimes applying pressure if she asked me to do so, she could anchor into the memories and begin to scream. It was a way of discovering the connections between the physical pain and the traumatic life experience that generated the blocked energy. This is one point where we may also become aware of the presence of an energy attachment.

As helpers, it is our responsibility to explore alternative techniques that fit each client situation. For example, sometimes Tia asked us to wrap her as tightly as possible in a king-sized sheet, arms down at her sides. Certainly, most people would feel constrained and unsafe in this situation, but for Tia, it was comforting to her and helped her feel safe. Being so tightly wrapped allowed Tia to move rage energy without being afraid she might hurt someone in the process. Our trained staff uses this technique only in rare and extreme situations, and always with the full awareness and permission of the client. The client retains full control and power to discontinue the process at any point.

Some clients need pressure on a specific area of the body. One of our clients struggled to get in touch with his emotions during a weekend workshop. By his third processing session, he knew he needed help to go deep enough to experience the relief he desired. Because he was in a relationship that made him feel trapped, he asked the facilitators and observers in the room to lie down on him. We placed a mat on top of him, then three people lay down across the mat, creating pressure equivalent to the pressure he was putting on himself. That physical weight helped him to access his repressed emotions about feeling trapped. This practice needs to be done with extreme care, of course. The client's airway is never to be covered, and the client remains in control of the session through constant dialogue with the lead facilitator. The client may ask for increased pressure or ask people to back off and get up. This is always done with the permission and direction of the client. The clear intent is always for healing.

During episodes of her abuse, Tia experienced being grabbed by her ankles and dragged. When she was describing the experience during a session, I asked her if she wanted someone to pull her ankles to help her go deeper. Initially, Tia requested that no one touch or go near her ankles during her processes. We had always carefully honored this request. This time, Tia said, "Yes, I feel like it could really help me move the energy connected to the times my perpetrators grabbed my ankles." Following Tia's lead, the application of tension at her ankles helped her move the energy and heal from this part of her trauma. This is one example of how we always honor and follow the lead of the client.

As the facilitator, you might ask the client if any props are needed to help the body express its truth in a physical way, thus moving stored energy. A facilitator can hold a pad that the participant hits with a plastic bat, or the participant can pull on a pole to create tension. No matter what method we use to help the client express truth and move energy, we continually check in by inquiring, "What are you experiencing in this moment?"

Tips for Facilitating Participatory Soul Retrieval

During an RTT session, one of the facilitator's responsibilities is recognizing when a client might need help for their inner wisdom or higher self to come forth and speak truth. When soul parts are too terrified to move or to speak, when they have been trapped in a traumatic event, we need to encourage the client's own wisdom in creating a safe space for the spell to be broken. When the client's higher self crosses over the perceived barrier and gently tells the child or young person, "I am here now," "You can do this," or "I am not going to leave you," it helps the trapped soul part step forward. Some of this is illustrated in Tia's session in chapter 4. This encouragement from the true, higher self helps break the spell of endless terror for the lost soul part.

Sometimes, it only takes one word for the child to break through the frozen, terrified state of being. As a facilitator, witness, or helper, we then ask the client if they see the light of the soul part. If they do, we suggest they say, "Come to me now. Come home." Once again, we remind the client to breathe, as a means of anchoring this soul part fully into his/her heart center and the body. As helpers, we also remind participants of the importance of creating their own ceremony or ritual to honor the lost soul parts that have come home.

Sometimes, the client is angry with the soul part and needs to be guided out of that anger. For example, one of our clients was angry with his eleven-year-old self who experienced an embarrassing incident, the memory of which continued to embarrass the client and cause him a great deal of insecurity throughout his life. That anger, however, only kept him separated from his eleven-year-old soul part and didn't allow for soul retrieval. His true anger was toward the people who made fun of him as a result of the embarrassing incident.

In his RTT session, the client was able to step aside and let the little boy part rage at his abusers. Once this energy was released, the client experienced a sense of calm and saw clearly that his anger was misdirected. He was then able to express compassion for the boy and apologize for his misdirected anger. In doing so, the soul parts reunited.

Facilitators have to assess the readiness of both the client and the soul part to reunite. Sometimes, the client does not feel worthy of having his/her soul part return. Other times, the client's heart is not yet fully open to the soul part. If this is the case, the soul part will not enter the body at that time. Facilitators may need to dialogue with the client and determine if this is the case. If so, they must reassure the client that there is no judgment, no right or wrong, with what they are experiencing and the choice they have made. Encouragement should be given that soul integration can happen at another time. The client's awareness of the soul part is a huge step in the healing journey.

A dialogue between the soul part and the client can be very helpful during RTT—speaking truth and hearing the soul part's truth. Our soul parts may not fully trust us because they feel abandoned. It can take some time and patience to convince them that it's safe to return home. As facilitators, we can encourage clients to have this dialogue and help them ask questions of their soul parts if they are struggling with the conversation.

At times, people experience flashbacks to the moment of shock when the soul part left the body. In this situation, the facilitator can assist with reframing and bringing closure to the oppressive experience by encouraging the client to speak truth to those who hurt him/her.

Soul parts enter into a natural reintegration process as the client breathes and relaxes. The manner in which soul parts present themselves for retrieval/reintegration varies for each person. Some may have a visual experience in which they see their soul parts as clearly as if they were watching a play on a stage. Others may experience what has been described as a translucent vision of themselves at younger ages. Still others experience forms or fields of light, while some have a purely energetic experience and a keen sense of energy returning.

When closing the soul retrieval part of the session, it's helpful for the client to use the same phrasing we sometimes recommend for maintenance: "This is 2016 (or whatever the current year happens to be). This is a new day. All that you shared and expressed did happen. It is not happening now. It is safe for you to come home. Home is right here in this body, which belongs to you and to me. This is your home, too. It's time for you to come home." The facilitator may now encourage the integration to occur by saying something like "Take deep breaths. Really breathe deep now. Breathe that soul part in." The client will then experience a return of the soul energy.

Closing the Session

It's important not to rush a client into finishing an RTT session. When he/she seems ready, the support person can remove the participant's blindfold, cautioning him/her not to open their eyes right away because the light will seem very bright after the total darkness of the blindfold. Provide a tissue for the client to wipe his/her eyes. Gradually, the client comes back to present space and time.

As you close the session, encourage the client to make full, sustained eye contact with you. This helps anchor him or her in the newfound safety and trust of another human being. Allow the client some space and time to integrate and relax.

Clients may notice that their breathing is much easier after an RTT session. It is important to alert the client to the fact that they have opened an inner doorway to energy movement. It's natural for that energy to want to continue in motion. Therefore the client may need to continue speaking truth to someone, to practice feeling their feelings instead of repressing them. They also need to know that their support person is available to them for continued processing if the need arises.

At White Raven Center, we hear clients express a desire to maintain their calm state indefinitely. The truth is we never know how many sessions will be required or how many soul parts will be discovered on our healing journey. What we do know is that with the return and integration of our soul parts, we give ourselves the gift of being fully present in this lifetime.

Closure happens when the client makes eye contact with each person present in the room. The witnesses then offer the client their own experience of having observed that individual's process. The client is generally more conscious and present after his/her process. Hearing the witnesses validate the client's experience emphasizes that they are not alone in their suffering—or their healing. If in a workshop setting, the lead facilitator then helps bring the session to a close by summarizing the experience and leading a discussion that elicits new awarenesses and insights from everyone present.

We encourage clients to linger in the post-RTT euphoric state for as long as they feel the need. Encourage the client to stay conscious of physical sensations and emotions over the days and even weeks following the session, and to use the maintenance techniques in this book to keep the energy moving and the soul parts anchored.

"Be the change you wish to see in the world."

—Mahatma Gandhi

Chapter 12

Healing Our Selves to Contribute to Healing the World

When people begin to heal through the RTT modality, they commonly ask the same question: "Why isn't everyone doing this?" We get excited about our ability to transform and want to share it with others. This is what I experienced after my first deep emotional healing process nineteen years ago. True healing transforms our ability to see not only the beauty that lies in each and every soul around us, but also the pain and suffering that people unconsciously choose to suppress every day. This new awareness can create a sense of dissonance and cause a feeling of urgency to change the world.

More commonly, it is simply a phase that most who wake up to the power of transformation go through. When we wake up, it's natural to desire to wake others up too, especially those we love. Gradually, we come to see that for some reason, not everyone truly desires healing and transformation. We learn to accept where others are on their journey and trust that each person ultimately knows what is best for himself or herself. We start practicing discernment as we witness others without judgment, expectation, or pressure to change.

One truth you may discover on this healing path is that the only thing you can truly change is yourself. With human witness, we begin to recognize that our minds want to drag us into complicated scenarios while our hearts encourage us just to *be*. Just being is simple and, in this state, we experience a sense of calm and are open to the joys of being fully in life. We accomplish our goal of inner peace and, in doing so, contribute significantly to peace in our families, communities, and the world.

The Freedom to Choose

The clients who come to the White Raven Center have arrived at a place in their lives where they feel that they must do something to heal; they can no longer bear the pain. The self-limiting beliefs that have created their suffering were absorbed in childhood. As children, they were not given a choice. Now, as adults, they do have a choice. We tell them they do not have to suffer anymore and that, through the RTT process, they will gift themselves the freedom to choose a life that nurtures their soul. Floyd says, "When we choose to heal, we join a society of those who have been given a second chance."

This brings to mind a story one of our clients shared about a dear friend of his. He had been trying to get his friend to face his pain and come to a workshop at White Raven Center to begin his healing process. When our client had conversations with his friend about it, however, the friend was passive, never quite saying "no," but never quite saying "yes" either. His friend acknowledged that he was suffering and even acknowledged that he needed help and that healing was possible. Yet, every time he was presented with an opportunity to take action, something else took priority.

This is a common story in our world, and it is a tragic story. As our client told us, "It's like my friend is enduring death by paper cuts."

The truth is, our client's friend hasn't suffered enough. As sad as that may be for our client, he must honor his friend's right to choose and trust that his friend's journey will unfold in perfect harmony with his divine plan. Carl Jung said, "There is no coming to consciousness without pain. People will do anything, no matter how absurd, in order to avoid facing their own soul. One does not become enlightened by imagining figures of light, but by making the darkness conscious." This is why the term "rock bottom" is used in addiction circles so often. There seems to be a concrete space inside everyone; once they arrive there, they will go no further but instead, at that poignant moment, they will begin to heal.

Many of the clients who come to the White Raven Center have come to that internal space—and that place is different for everyone. Many are ready to die. Some have endured a tragedy, and it has ignited a desire for change. Some people just have their eyes more open than others, can see the destructive patterns in their lives and where those patterns are taking them, and have the courage to make the change before the suffering becomes unbearable.

Breaking the Cycle

This is where we see the human beings whose past actions unconsciously control our lives every day. They may be our fathers, our uncles, our mothers, our cousins, our teachers, our brothers, our sisters, and more—all who used pain and fear to teach us about life. To illustrate, as previously said, we expect unconditional love and acceptance from our parents when we are children. We are born feeling fully entitled to this, and we are indeed entitled to it. Yet, in our infant state, we have no appreciation of our parents as individuals in their own process of learning with their own fears, traumas, and wounds. We naturally take all of their choices personally and are wounded by them.

Because of this, when we experience traumatic events or recurrent experiences of disappointment, frustration or judgment from our parents or others, we feel victimized. We feel backed into a corner with no way out, and the mental and emotional pressures can be overwhelming. That's when parts of us detach in order to survive. What replaces them are toxic energies that carry internal belief systems. This energy cycles back to itself the beliefs (or charge) it carries. Thus the internal reality survives in a sort of holding cycle until the suffering is too great, at which point we begin to move the energy and interrupt the cycle.

Our client Nicole told us how car problems seemed to be a curse in her life. It seemed that no matter what she did, any vehicle she would purchase would break down on her in the most ridiculous ways. As she began to do her RTT work, she started to see that this experience of being cursed was a manifestation of her internal belief system, programmed by her family. And her car breaking down was actually an energetic manifestation of a deep internal belief—intense self-hatred stemming from a childhood filled with neglect and abuse from her primary caretakers.

No matter how much she would try to think positively about her situation, the "curse" would eventually manifest. A part of her internally yearned to be provided for, protected, and loved; another part of her believed she deserved nothing but hardship, struggle, and poverty. As Nicole came to these realizations, she also noticed the toxic cycles in her friendships and family relationships. The universe, it seemed, was always angry with Nicole, and she was required to suffer continuously in toxic relationships, jobs she hated, and broken-down vehicles in order to pay for her crimes and appease her family of origin.

When Nicole started to move her core emotional energy, her car problems were the first thing to end. As if she had removed a large boulder from a river, the waters began to run more smoothly. She became free to ask questions about the other unwanted things in her life. The drama in her relationships began to lessen because she no longer asked others to change, and she began to see the world around her as her teacher—there to reveal what she could not see in her own life. This shift in her consciousness has raised her vibration and broken the destructive cycle she felt trapped in; that healing has inevitably had a positive impact on the world around her.

Becoming Peace

Nicole is an example of what occurs when we connect with inner peace. Suddenly, the world around us reflects that harmonious state back to us. When we stand back and observe our world, we can all see that this principle of transforming the self in order to transform those around us functions on the universal level as well. Will Durant said, "A civilization can only be destroyed outwardly when it has already destroyed itself inwardly." If this is the case, then it is equally true that no civilization will outwardly live in peace until every citizen has inwardly established his or her own inner sense of peace.

My life experiences tell me that to become peace, I must consciously engage in an inward journey. At times this can feel anything but peaceful, as I allow others to trigger places within me where disharmony hides. As I learn to become an observer of my own process, to not judge or blame, to forgive others and myself, a sense of calm opens to me. This transformation requires that we make a commitment to having peace in our lives. It requires us to be willing to acknowledge that others are our mirrors and that they continually reflect back to us our own state of peace or disharmony. It also requires that we take action outwardly to support those systems and programs that promote peace in our world.

Rapid Transformation Therapy

To achieve peace we start by setting our intent, which will affect all levels, phases, and spheres of our vast universe. Efforts made on the physical, mental, emotional, spiritual, social, environmental, and global spheres serve as catalysts for growth on every other level of being and existence. Just as we recycle products to protect the environment and keep it clean, we concurrently cleanse our body, mind, and spirit.

As a civilization, we are at a critical time on our planet when humans are being called to heal the emotional body. This can help create peace and healing for the entire world—not just humans, but all beings and systems. Again, the soul is not static. We are either choosing a path of healing and peace or a path of self-destruction.

"Let us fill our hearts with our own compassion—
toward ourselves and toward all living beings."

—Thich Nhat Hanh

Love Energy

Ultimately, when we speak of anything being transformed more into the likeness of its truest nature, we are speaking about love. The energy of love is the most powerful healing ingredient that exists throughout our universe. It is the most plentiful, affordable, and reliable source of medicine that we have. Healing ourselves is really about reconnecting with the love that lives inside of us and releasing the natural flow of love energy. It's about connecting with our essence—our source. Love is the substance that gives life to all things.

Often, when clients come to the White Raven Center, they walk away having experienced love for the first time. They not only experience love through the interactions they have with other human beings at the center; they learn how to open their hearts to the higher vibration of love. Our workshops create an environment where participants connect to the love that lives inside of them as they heal, and to the love inside the other people around them.

Together, we all become partners in a community of people healing alongside each other. The more we replicate this in the world, the more we will contribute to world peace. Imagine what our world would be like if we asked the simple question, "What does love have to say about it?" when faced with any perplexing problem or life challenge.

An Invitation

I wrote this book with enormous support from my husband and our White Raven team, to show that there is a way out of limiting core beliefs. Because of the work we have done on ourselves, we understand the insanity of suffering and of pain. We understand that the core of our issues comes from this society, which continues to teach what it does not truly understand.

Our society is like an entity that attaches to us and feeds on us, needing to be in control. It tries to make us believe that it has all the answers and tells us there is only one way . . . and that way is to not feel. This entity knows our basic nature is to love, to be happy, to feel joy, and to feel peace. This entity cannot control us when we find ourselves in a positive state of being; it uses any means necessary to keep us confused. And it always starts with an immature, innocent, naive child. This entity does not care. It only knows that if you wake up to the truth about who you truly are, it will lose control of you. That terrifies this entity. It knows that it needs the energy of many human beings to continue being in control.

When the child is able to speak truth, to express his/her feelings, it no longer feels and hears this entity. The entity knows this, so it intensifies the electrical charge. It brings more like-minded entities to totally shut down the child, and the child understands at some level that something is wrong. Yet, because the charge is so great, the child turns this energy on himself or herself and continues walking on the path dictated by this entity, all the way into adulthood. Then, one day, the child within snaps and screams, "No more! I can't do this anymore!" At that moment a light goes on, and a call goes out to the universe for help. The negative charge becomes positive, for this child feels there must be another way of living than the way he or she has been forced to live.

We at the White Raven Center have all been that child. We have seen these children and know these children when they walk into our center. The feeling of love, of mother/father energy, of being nurtured, of being welcomed, comes from within ourselves. At the White Raven Center, we have witnessed the miracle of many children taking back their power, escaping the control of this entity, and walking the path that they are truly meant to follow in this life.

We have been witnesses to rapid transformation every day. We see people learning to feel again, resurrecting long-dormant aspects of their creative self with such speed and effectiveness that I still find myself constantly surprised by it. Every single day, we watch people—who have seemingly only known hurt in their lives—step into better futures as they allow peace to walk hand-in- hand with their suffering.

We see trauma make way for joy, rage make way for calm, and despair make way for intimacy and connection. We see people at various places on the path to freedom, as some desire it more intensely than others. Some have more courage and curiosity. Some bring themselves to awareness fully, and some still hide. Yet there is always change, because the spirit that drives the healing of the world can be trusted.

RTT is a spirit-driven therapeutic modality. It stands as a testimony to the idea that we are not segmented beings, divided in our physical, spiritual, emotional, and mental bodies. It is truly an evolutionary step in the marriage of spirit and psyche. We invite you to take the step now and move into the practice of this modality, and we are grateful to be a part of your experience of transformation. May you be blessed on your journey.

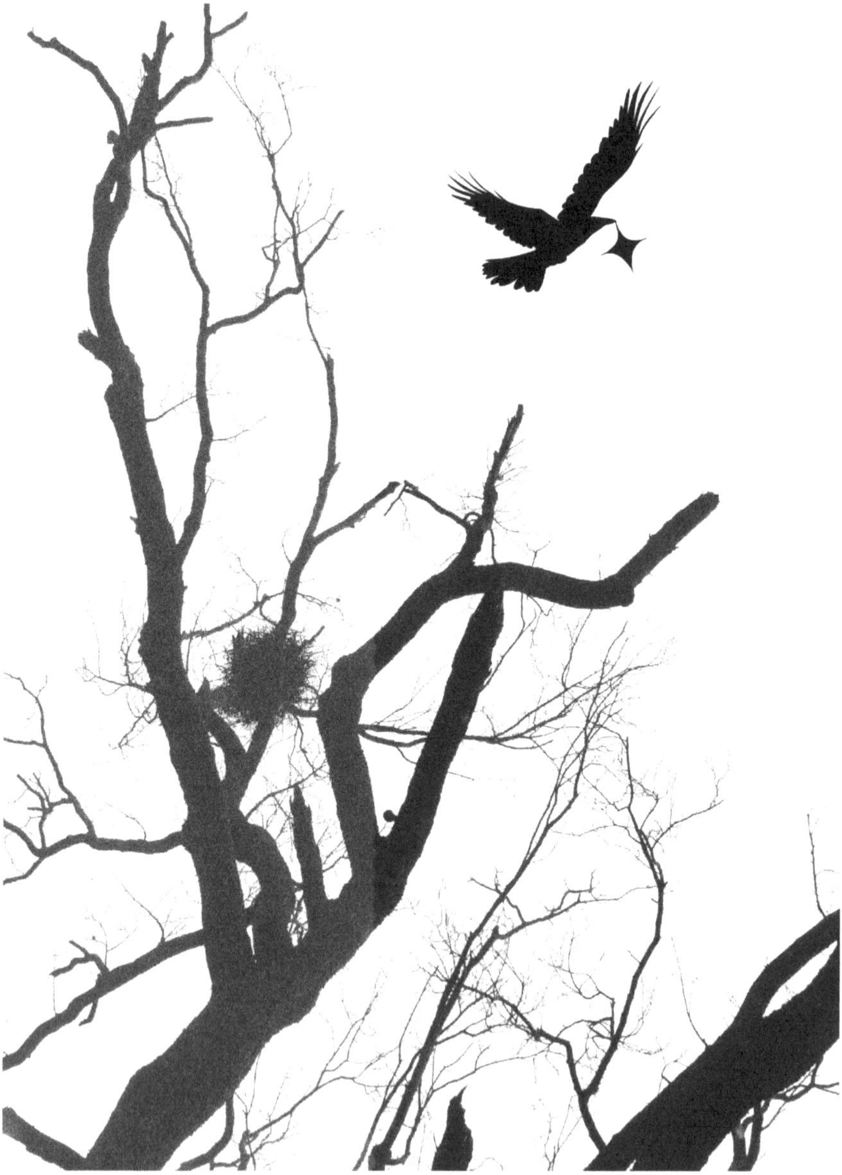

Appendix A

RTT's Connection to Other Treatment Modalities/Theories

If you trace the advancement of therapeutic modalities from their early days in the late 1800s (when psychology was formalized as a field of study) to today's more integrated perspectives of the self, you will see that there is a story being told. The narrative arc seems to be moving toward fully integrated therapeutic modalities. Today's world requires modalities that bring more than self- knowledge, or that merely allow us to control our anxiety and depression and suffering. There must be more than medicinal fixes available to the human soul. And so it seems that people are returning to the spirit, just as scientists are starting to realize that mystery and spirit might be at the heart of all of life—that everything is energy and everything is one.

It is time for therapies that integrate the entire self to be labeled as something more than "alternative." They are more rightly understood as practices born from the most basic foundations of the human experience.

RTT is effective because it integrates the entire self and allows people to wake up to the union of psyche and spirit. The spirit, soul, emotions, mind/psyche, and physical body—viewed as one seamless and integrated body—need not be parceled out and disconnected in a way that requires us to address one piece or another. Instead, RTT aims at the fundamental root of a person's being and unlocks their ability to heal the whole self. This root can be understood as spirit or soul—the ether in which every part of our being and creation floats.

Until recently, it seems that spirit was more widely thought of in our culture as something like magic—something transcendent rather than something that is, at its base, most fully human. In this age, as many religions release their tight grip on people and more and more human beings seek real transformation and a true end to the anxiety and depression that seem to haunt our species, spirit is emerging from behind the shroud that some religions cast over it for centuries. The psychological world is taking notice of the shift. Modalities like RTT are being born in this new age.

At the White Raven Center, we have clients who are themselves practicing therapists. Our clients include doctors and social workers, massage therapists, and teachers—healers of all sorts. They all come here with various wounds and, through the techniques discussed in this book, begin a new process of allowing their spirits to root out the pain trapped in their bodies. They recover the parts of their souls that have been scattered across time and space. They move beyond belief and control, into a new paradigm of the world and themselves.

RTT, however, is not the only type of therapy that employs this new perspective of the world and of healing. I offer this appendix to briefly describe some of the other types of therapy that have been born from this perspective of the integrated self. All of these types of therapy have a few things in common. They take seriously the ancient concepts of how energy flows through the human body and its effects on the internal self, as well as the world around the individual. They are all concerned with matters of consciousness, repressed pain, and trauma.

Each of these modalities is focused on true healing—a transformation of how one feels every day, rather than just a type of knowledge that allows a person to control his/her suffering. I want to discuss these therapies with the idea that there is more than one way to approach your suffering therapeutically, and many of them are related to each other. Yet, whichever way you choose to approach it, you will be required to work inward.

Eye Movement Desensitization and Reprocessing (EMDR)

EMDR is a type of psychotherapy designed to use the body's natural healing processes to address PTSD. As a clinician moves the client through the phases of treatment, they begin by using eye movement and other bilateral stimulation in conjunction with certain painful memories. The client holds these specific memories in mind as the therapist moves his/her hand laterally across the client's field of vision. The client tracks the therapist's hand with his/her eyes. As the client focuses on the movement of the therapist's hand, repressed memories surface and stored emotions are triggered. The activation of memories and emotions allows the client to process trauma as it releases affiliated energy. Much like the soul retrieval process, EMDR therapy is effective in shifting the internal meaning a person possesses in reference to a memory or an event in the past. Often, after EMDR processing, a person is able to say, "It happened, but it's not happening anymore, and I am stronger and calmer than before."

Lifespan Integration Therapy

Lifespan Integration is another body-based healing modality that allows one's own natural healing processes the freedom to do what they were designed to do. When undergoing LI therapy, a client is guided to create and use a timeline of life memories in order to help access the trauma stored in the body/mind associated with these times.

If trauma creates a fragmented soul, integrating these various aspects of self is the key to being able to reorient oneself to life and the painful memories one may hold from past traumas. LI facilitates that integration much like a slow walk through one's life, with the body's stored energy coming up along the way. As these stored emotions are experienced, the memories of past trauma can be integrated into the overall experience of life and a person can be restored to himself or herself.

Family System/Attachment-Based Therapies

These therapeutic approaches are based on the idea that just as trauma occurs within the relational system of our families, so does healing. They are designed to root out where the roles we were taught to play—and the pain associated with those roles—have moved into the unconscious and are causing suffering. Healing in one of these types of modalities comes in the form of creating healthy attachments with the self (sometimes through guided "re- birthing" processes) and then consequently in the relationships around you.

Regression Therapy/Hypnosis

Hypnosis is a useful way of penetrating the barriers that the self has built to protect it from feeling repressed memories and pain. Regression therapists will often employ hypnosis in order to expose the memories that still exist in the unconscious and are causing unwanted suffering. Sometimes these memories will reveal themselves as having their root in past lives, which can be healed as well. Brian L. Weiss's groundbreaking book, *Many Lives, Many Masters*, tells the story of a client who began healing past life wounds through regression therapy.

Jungian Theory

The psychologist Carl Jung (1875–1961) did some of history's most groundbreaking work on how unconscious pain dominates the lives of human beings. His theories built on the work of Sigmund Freud and focused on the struggle between the various parts of the ego. A therapist employing Jungian theory will help you analyze the symbolism in your waking visions and dreams, which in turn point to the unconscious pain that is causing unwanted suffering.

Energy-Based Therapies

There are many types of therapeutic techniques that are fundamentally centered on the movement of energy in the body. Some examples of these are:

Emotional Freedom Technique (EFT)—A technique that uses focused tapping on the body's energy meridian points to access trapped energy and integrate painful memories.

Acupuncture—An acupuncturist inserts thin needles into energy meridian points in the body; these needles help release trapped energy. This staple of traditional Chinese medicine is deeply relaxing and effective.

Energy and Mindfulness Meditation—Ultimately, all of these theories are based on the concept that all things are made up of the same energy. Meditating on this idea can have remarkable transformative effects. Again, this is based on the idea that the body/mind/spirit is designed to heal itself. The specifics of mindfulness practices vary; most often, they are driven by guided imagery (imagining all things becoming energy), then allowing the spiritual truth of this to be experienced.

Shamanic Healing—The ancient practices and ceremonies of most indigenous cultures required that a shaman (sometimes referred to as a medicine man or medicine woman) journey to the spiritual realms for the healing of the tribe. Each region and tribe has contextual nuances in their understanding and application of shamanistic principles—but in all contexts, shamanism remains a spiritually based method of moving energy. These practices, like many of the modalities discussed above, are integrated into the experience of healing found at the White Raven Center, and are also becoming a more widely known and accepted technique of rapid healing.

There is more that can be said regarding therapeutic modalities that deal with unconscious, repressed energy/pain. However, our intent here is simply to show how RTT is an integrated modality that carries pieces of all of these theories with it. Ultimately, when the spirit is allowed to direct the healing process, the healing theories and techniques that emerge all have deep similarities. For instance, if all human beings trap energy inside of their bodies when they are emotionally wounded, then any theory that is effective will lead to that truth—though the path to that point may vary in look and feel. One thing that can be definitively said about each of these therapeutic methods is that they provide quick, noticeable transformations.

The advancement of spiritually and energetically integrated therapeutic modalities is gradually silencing the archaic thinking that healing takes either vast amounts of time or simply will never be reached. Modern people are asking deeper questions of those who claim to possess the ability to heal. There seems to be a requirement emerging that 1) it works, and 2) it brings more than intellectual awareness of various issues and histories.

Healing Our Selves to Contribute to Healing the World

 Many people today are willing to dive deeper into self and are seeking an advanced level of consciousness. For that to happen, we have to free ourselves from the behaviors and experiences that cause us suffering.

Appendix B

Floyd's White Raven Story

As mentioned in the prologue, the White Raven story is told in many different ways. This is one of Floyd's versions.

One day, as Raven was flying above the southern tip of Southeast Alaska, he heard his name spoken. A storyteller down below had just begun to tell the story of Raven. It was evening, but Raven could see smoke rising out of the thick canopy of yellow cedar trees. Down he was drawn to the fire surrounded by human beings.

Raven noticed that most of those who were listening to the storyteller were young people. All of them were staring at the man in anticipation. The storyteller pointed at the stars in the sky with a stick and said, "Raven put the stars up there."

The man had timed his story just as the moon began to rise over the surrounding mountains. "See the moon? Raven brought that, too. And in the morning, when we see the light from the sun? Remember that Raven brought it to us to melt the darkness away. Now, you ask, why would Raven do that?"

The young people nodded their heads. They wanted to know why Raven would do that. The audience, including Raven himself, settled in to hear the rest of the story. The man continued:

Well, Raven is just like you and me. He needs us, and we need him. You see, a long time ago, Raven was alone. He was so lonely. Now, how could that be, you ask? He is a creator, isn't he?

Yes, that's true, but Raven has feelings just like you and me.

Healing Our Selves to Contribute to Healing the World

And even though he wasn't the only Raven, he didn't spend time with the others. Their home was in the sky, flying alone. So Raven decided to visit the world below him called Earth. He flew through a hole in the sky and straight down into a world of darkness—a world where there were no stars, no moon, no sun.

It was so quiet—no sound. Raven realized he was hungry—he was always hungry and could fill his belly up so much that he couldn't move—so he landed on a beach to look for food. He walked along the shore kicking over rocks to look for clams or fish trapped in a tide pool. Then, suddenly, he heard a scream. He looked up toward the sky, he looked across the water, he looked around the beach. But he saw nothing.

Raven heard the scream again. The sound was coming from down by one of his claws. He turned his head toward the sand to get a better look and there, climbing back into a clam shell, were these tiny human beings. They were scrambling to get back into that shell in order to hide, but it was crowded in there. Some of them stared up at Raven with terror in their eyes.

Raven was curious about these creations, but he realized that to them, he was a giant bird. So he decided to shrink himself down to the size of the ravens we see today. Then he waddled up to these humans to study them. At his new size, they were no longer afraid of him.

As Raven looked closer at these new creations, he became aware that they didn't have feathers like a bird. They had no fangs to protect themselves either. They had no fur to protect them from the harsh weather. Some of them were already shivering from the cold.

They aren't going to make it without help, Raven thought. So, with a sense of urgency, he shifted back to his giant self and cawed to Eagle, to Bear, to Wolf, and to Salmon. They all came, and they gathered around this clamshell containing the first human beings. Eagle looked at them and said, "They have no feathers! And with those small eyes, they can't see far. No beak either!"

Bear said, "They have no fur, no claws!"

Wolf said, "I noticed that, too. And they can't see in the dark.

That isn't good."

Salmon said, "They have no fins, and their skin is so thin that they will soon freeze to death."

All agreed that this new creation of human beings, if not given help, would never make it in this world. So Raven asked, "What shall we do?"

"Well," Eagle said, "I will allow them to use my feathers."

"I will allow them to use my fur," Bear said.

"I, too, will allow them to use my fur," Wolf agreed.

"And I will come back every summer to the rivers to provide food for them," Salmon added.

All looked at each other and agreed. "We will help these human beings. We only have one request—that they will always respect us."

The first human beings did not understand this discussion. All the human beings heard was growling and cawing. Raven looked at the human beings and realized they needed to understand this request. *I will tell them after they awaken to their abilities to create,* he decided. He saw them in that moment like caterpillars that had just broken out of their cocoon and were learning how to live on this earth.

★★★

The storyteller paused for a moment and looked at the children with serious eyes. One day, he told them, a human being disrespected and ignored this agreement. As a result, we humans lost the ability to communicate with these creatures. But that is another story . . .

Healing Our Selves to Contribute to Healing the World

The storyteller turned his head to look at Raven, who was not far away making guttural sounds toward him. The man smiled at Raven and then turned back to the children and said, "Did you know that Raven was white? He shone like a light. What happened, you ask, to turn Raven black?" And then, the storyteller continued his story:

Well, the original human beings were no more than animals. "This is not right," thought Raven. "It isn't right for these creations to live in darkness either." So Raven walked to the shore near the water and thought about what to do. After a time of thinking, he turned and walked back to the human beings and stared at them. He looked at the ocean and thought, "What can I do to make the ocean shrink so that these humans can harvest the clams, octopus, seaweed, and fish? What can I put up in the sky so that they can find their way at night? What can I place in the sky that will help them to build a shelter, to hunt, and to fish?"

When he looked at how innocent the humans were, he thought, "Light! That's what needs to be placed in their hearts so that they can create for themselves! I do not want them to be so dependent on us."

At that moment he had an idea, so he spread his wings and flew back through the hole in the sky, back to the land of his birth. You see, he knew of a family that ate, walked, talked, and dressed like human beings but lived their lives in the sky. They had only one season, and that was summer. They had no darkness. When they were tired, they would go into their long house and make it pitch black so that they could sleep. They had no need of anything, as they created whatever they wanted.

Raven considered what he knew about this family and remembered that the chief had treasures that he kept in three boxes. These treasures were for the chief's entertainment and pleasure—things to play with. These treasures were the chief's prize possessions, and they had the power to save the helpless human beings.

But how would Raven get into the long house to get the treasures? The family knew the trickster that Raven was, and they didn't trust him. You see, he had a tendency to eat and eat and eat until there was nothing left, so Raven was never invited into their home.

Raven watched the house . . . and waited . . . watched . . . and waited . . . until one day, he noticed that the chief's daughter had a habit of walking down to the river with a cup in her hand to get a drink of water. She placed the cup in the water and took a drink. Now, you must realize that Raven can shift into any form he desires. So he turned himself into a tiny cedar needle and floated himself down the river, directly toward the cup that the chief's daughter placed in the water. She swept up the water without noticing the cedar needle, and she drank it. The next thing she knew, she became pregnant. You might think the family would be surprised by this event, but they were not. In fact, they were happy that another child was coming into their world.

But they were indeed surprised that in just a matter of days, the chief's daughter gave birth to a boy who started walking on his very first day. And he was oh, so hungry. But the chief was so happy with his grandson that he demanded they continue feeding him what he wanted. Still, no matter how much they fed him, it was never enough.

Secretly, the baby followed his grandfather chief and watched as the chief opened the three boxes. A brilliant light filled the room. The baby cried, making himself known to his grandfather and pointing at the boxes. He wanted to play with the balls of light. Grandfather covered his ears to muffle the high-pitched screech of his grandson, but he relented to the child's demands. "Only one box," Grandfather said.

Grandfather opened the first box and released the stars that danced around his grandson. The baby laughed with glee as the little globes of light circled around him. Finally, Grandfather said, "That's enough," and he took the stars and placed them back into the box.

Later that night, the baby snuck into the room and opened the box of stars. As he did so, he changed himself back into Raven, swept the stars into his beak, flew through the door, and back to the hole that led down to earth. Down he flew, opening his beak and slowly scattering the stars throughout the sky.

Raven flew back down to the human beings and noticed that they were still hiding in their clamshell, still hungry and cold. Back through the hole in the sky flew Raven and back to the chief's house, changing himself once again into the form of a spoiled child. When the chief awoke and walked over to check on his treasures, he screamed when he noticed that his stars were gone. Everyone looked and looked for the stars, but they could not find them.

Grandfather was so disappointed. Still, he had his moon to enjoy. But his grandson wanted to play with this ball, too. And again, when the baby screeched, the grandfather covered his ears and placated the child by allowing him to play with the precious moon. Once again, after some time, Grandfather told his grandson that it was time for bed, took the moon, and gently placed it back into the box.

Raven waited and waited until everyone was asleep. He crept back to the box, changed into his bird form, and reached into the box with his beak. Then he flew out of the house, back through the hole that opened to the earth with the brilliantly lit moon in his mouth. When he released it, it floated and settled into the sky. Raven glanced down at the human beings and noticed they were still hiding in their clamshell, still confused, still hungry, and still cold. Raven turned and flew back through the hole in the sky back to the home of his grandfather, who awoke and noticed that the lid to the box holding the moon was open. He screamed, waking everyone up, and again, they searched to no avail. The moon was nowhere to be found.

So Grandfather became extremely protective of his last treasure—the sun. He even guarded the door of the house.

Raven did not cry and try to play with the sun. He simply waited until everyone was asleep and quietly walked over to the last box, transforming into his Raven self. When he flipped over the lid, however, the light was so bright that it woke everyone up. Raven had to quickly grab the sun in his beak and fly up toward the smokehole in the roof since the door was guarded. As Raven squeezed through the smokehole, black soot completely covered his white feathers. In that moment, Raven transformed into the black raven we see around us today.

Below him, he heard the screams of his grandfather, who had come to realize that Raven had deceived him. Off Raven flew to the hole leading to Earth, and down the hole he went, opening his beak to release the sun above the Earth. Immediately, the darkness disappeared.

Raven flew down to the first human beings. He noticed that they were glowing from within. He could see a little sun in their hearts, and he was happy, for they were leaving the clamshell to seek shelter and food.

✷✷✷

A smile came to the storyteller's face as he turned to see the Raven fly away, cawing loudly. The man turned to the children and said, "Now, you know why we respect Raven. He had so much compassion for humankind that he sacrificed a part of himself, forgetting who he really was, and accepting the shadow of darkness. It is said that one day, after a long period of darkness, humankind will awaken and reconnect with their spirituality. When that happens, Raven will return to his original pure white form."

In the last twenty years, there have been sightings of ravens whose feathers are turning white in the Yukon-Kuskokwim Delta and Southeast Alaska. Today, white ravens are well-known to the people of the Queen Charlotte Islands. Many tribes believe that Raven is a messenger from the spirit world, a bringer of light who connects us to our true spirits, to unconditional love for ourselves and all of humankind.

Rapid Transformation Therapy

Appendix C

A Reflection From an RTT Participant

Friend and co-worker, Zach Fairbanks recently shared with me the following poem written after his first weekend of RTT processing.

The Forest Speaks

My heart is open, I can hear

This land where I was born
this place I was raised
visions of my childhood
remembered by the trees who watched over me

The trails that carried along my joyful running feet
"Wait, Cheska,[12] wait for me."
Weaving through silent trunks
jumping bulging roots
I can see the happy bouncing boy
hear the happy joyous plea

Where have you been all these years my dear boy?
The trees seem to inquire
quiet and patient,
lovingly silent,
so utterly true.

---

[12] Cheska is Zach's older sister

Rapid Transformation Therapy

What during these few short years has happened to you?
you used to laugh at our falling leaves,
we used to play catch with the breeze,
we would sword fight as much as you pleased,
What? They implore,
has happened to you?

We are here.
Their presence speaks to me,
Let open your heart, let your sorrow be free.
Rest again in our fallen leaves,
touch our trunks,
climb amongst our branches,
feel the wind.

Yes, I know, you remember my joy.
The open free love I had as a boy.
I thank you so dearly,
FROM THE DEPTHS OF MY SOUL
for reminding me,
of the time I was whole

The pain in my heart had taken such hold
that to even my loved ones my heart had grown cold.
I have been in hiding, all of these years.
my heart locked up tight in a prison of torment

Fear whispering lies of the pain that must be,
you were wrong to love so openly.
And see what happened,
little boyo don't you see?
These people don't believe in love.
They worship me!

Healing Our Selves to Contribute to Healing the World

You best toe the line,
act the part,

feel the battle cry,
you best join with us my boy,
you know......you could die.
So like any draftee whose gig was up
I steeled my heart and took up the cup.

Though doors are tricky and I thank God for this fact
for love's foot kept that door open a crack.

Through all the fear, pain and despair
my soul always knew,
love is still there.
A wisp of cool air in the furnace's hot glare,
a drop of cool rain in the desert when no one was there.

This spark,
this tiny light in the darkness,
though it flickered and dimmed
to me it still harkens.
Brighter and brighter and brighter it's grown
door opening wider with each heartfelt groan
beautiful birches, Beith[13] calling me home.

I stand on the doorsill,
this liminal hold.
My presence is key to be safely this bold

My mind will step through, for my mind has forgot
though my body remembers the truth of fears lot.
To love this fully is to feel it all,

_____
[13] The Gaelic word for birch

Rapid Transformation Therapy

with no hesitation,
to answer the call.
I remember the pain
the fall from my grace.

Now as a man,
in a world apart.
How do I step through
with my open heart?
Yes, I know the answer,
and time it is taking.
As each step I take,
my body is quaking.

Tears they roll,
all down in streams.
I know truth,
move forward,
I lean.
And unto my self,
I have this thing to prove,

I worship love,
and through my heart alone.
I swear to Creator
My children will know love as their home!

The trees of their lives will tell different stories,
of children allowed to live on in their glory
of love living free and friendship retained,
a mother and father,
open hearts, passions flames.

Children of the Earth
sacred mother regained.
My heart is open
I can hear

The Forest Speaks
Zachariah McDonald Fairbanks
9/27/2010

Rapid Transformation Therapy

Appendix D

White Raven Center Tool Kit

Prior to an elder stepping out of his/her home, the elder checks within "self" to see if he/she is in balance, in a place of reverence, and takes a moment to say "Thank you, thank you, Creator. You have the way." When we are in ceremony, we are reminded that we are part of something greater. Over the years, we have added many ceremonies of the heart to our work at the White Raven Center.

Our elders taught us that when we do sacred healing work, we are entering the realm of ceremony. Ceremonies help remind us of who we truly are; in this place of gratitude, we connect with the light within. The intent of ceremony is to slow us down, to stop us from listening to the voice of the ego, and to enter the place of reverence. The following are some of the tools we have gathered and practice regularly, in private and as a group. We hope you find them useful.

COME FOR THE FOOD ~ STAY FOR THE HEALING

Part of sustaining good health is paying attention to the foods we eat. Preparing vibrant, colorful, healthy meals is a ceremony in itself. At White Raven Center, the meals we provide for participants have become a part of the healing process, as each dish is prepared with love and prayers. Our delicious meals have gained such a reputation that one of our facilitators

(Rebecca) coined the phrase you can now see displayed on our aprons: "Come for the Food ~ Stay for the Healing."

As we gather for meals, we always bless the food and give thanks for the many hands that have volunteered to help with meal preparation. I invite you to consider turning your meal preparation into a simple sacred ceremony.

THANKING OUR ANCESTORS

At the beginning of our weekend sessions, we acknowledge our ancestral helpers with a Haida chant taught to Floyd by artist Reggie Davidson. This song reminds us to give thanks to our helpers in the unseen world. Humbly, we stand before our ancestors and sing this song of gratitude and reverence. This simple ceremony helps us set the energy for the intensive weekend.

I AM THE BELOVED ~ I AM MY LOVE

On Saturday mornings at our monthly WRC workshops, we pair up and do an exercise called "I AM the beloved." A couple of years ago during one of our weekend sessions, Don Miguel Ruiz was in town. As a group, we all went to his Friday evening lecture. At the suggestion of one of our participants (Rebecca), we developed a variation of the exercise using Ruiz's words "I am my love." These words are powerful in either version, and provide a tool for participants to gauge where they are in relationship to self. If we resonate with these words, we know we are in a place of calm and self-love; we are in the now. For example, if Rebecca and Cathy were partnered for the ceremony, Cathy would say, "I am my love." Rebecca would then validate Cathy by saying, "Yes, Cathy, you are your love." If these words trigger strong emotions or feelings of avoidance and not belonging, we know there are places within us that remain fearful, self-doubting, and unworthy. These uncomfortable places serve as our inner guide, showing us where we need to work and move more energy.

We have one participant (Bee) who uses the words "I am the beloved" as a meditation while she walks her dog around a nearby lake. This simple tool allows her to release all the static energy of the day, to re-center herself, and to connect with her inner calm and self-love. As a witness to her exercise of truth, she calls upon the spirit of her grandmother guide. This helps anchor her soul energy in a place of love, as the feeling is mirrored by the essence and knowingness of grandmother's love.

PRACTICE DISCERNMENT

Learning what is a triggered emotion, what is an emotion of the moment, and what is an emotional response generated by gratitude are all part of learning discernment. Triggered emotions are never about what is going on in the moment. Emotions of the moment can be released freely and easily when you allow them to be expressed. Feelings of gratitude happen when the heart is open, and often arise when we rediscover our own deep connection to all that is.

Another part of discernment is learning to recognize if what I am feeling is really my own emotion or someone else's. For people who are very sensitive and spend considerable time out of their bodies, feelings may become very convoluted. There are numerous exercises to help them reconnect with their center. Some are very simple. By taking a few deep breaths and tapping on the energetic heart center, they can calm and come back into their center. It is from this place that they are able to discern what they are feeling in their bodies as truth for self or another. This can take lots of practice, or may come easily for some.

Another immediate way of centering your self—for the purpose of discernment—is something we call "be here now." Close your eyes, focus on your breath, draw in a deep, slow breath, and say to yourself slowly, "Be . . . here . . . NOW." Take a moment to notice how your body has relaxed and how you are now present in the moment.

KEEP IT SIMPLE

Our minds have a tendency to want to complicate everything. Remember to keep things simple. Use the "be here now" exercise to help you relinquish the complexity of the conscious mind. When you recognize the extent to which the ego mind wants to stay in control and instead allow yourself to keep things simple, you diminish the ego mind's power significantly.

I AM NOT MY EMOTIONS

When intense feelings become activated within your being, remember to say to yourself, "I am not my emotions. I am a divine light being." Emotions are merely energy forms that we do not want to get trapped in the body. Keep moving your emotions by speaking truth, sharing feelings, and asking for human witness when you feel out of balance.

BECOME THE OBSERVER

Practice becoming the observer of yourself and others. You are not your emotions, and you are not your ego mind. You can learn to observe your thoughts, feelings and behaviors. You can learn to observe others without getting pulled into their drama. By becoming an observer of all of life, you are free to enjoy it fully. As you anchor yourself as an observer in your center, functioning from a place of heart, you become a true expression of love.

FLIP THE SWITCH

As you learn to become an observer of your thoughts you can step back, stop fighting the thoughts, and "flip the switch." When you practice flipping the switch to the clarity and blessing of the moment, you can enjoy the calm that lies within you and create your heart's desires from that place. You then become conscious of how you expend so much energy focusing on the negative. Flipping the switch is about recognizing that you have a choice.

OUR THOUGHTS ARE OUR PRAYERS

Grandmother Falling Leaves would always say to her students, "Your thoughts are your prayers." Grandmother was suggesting that we become conscious of what we are thinking, because we can draw darkness into our lives with doom and gloom thoughts and beliefs. Prayers come from the heart, from a place of centeredness. When we are in that place, we direct our lives through intention. As we give thanks, we accept the gifts we desire as if they have already been given.

THE MIND KNOWS NOTHING ABOUT HEALING

When you participate in breath work, you may discover how much stress you put on your body. You might also discover that your ego mind is not your friend because it craves drama, needs control, and wants to prolong suffering. When you disconnect from the dialogue of the conscious mind through the breath, you discover the way of the heart. As this happens you connect to your wisdom and inner knowingness, which serve as guides to your healing.

THE BREATH

When you first focus consciously on your breath, notice *how* you are breathing. Are you swallow-breathing, are you holding your breath, or are you breathing like a baby naturally does, filling up your belly with oxygen? You may notice the distraction of the mind—a pull to focus on something else. Stay with the breath, and the mind will eventually give up and let go. The breath will guide you into your core issues and reveal the truth. Check in with your breath from time to time, especially if you are feeling anxious. When you experience anxiety, you are usually out of your body. Take a few deep breaths and draw your awareness back into the body. You will notice a sense of calm return to you. There is no life without the breath, and the breath is a powerful tool to help you restore balance.

TRUTH IS A POWERFUL HEALER

When you share truth with another human being, you both receive healing. Contained energy has been released, and a feeling of relief is the result. The human witness, together with the breathwork, will help you open the door of your inner truth. You might find yourself crying or feeling afraid because it feels like your pain is happening again. When you release the pain, you will discover the truth that your trauma did happen, but it is not happening now. Truth is a powerful healer. Practice sharing truth in the moment during your day-to-day life.

PRACTICE THE FOUR AGREEMENTS

Our team at the White Raven Center highly recommends incorporating into your daily practice the wisdom of the Toltec culture as resurrected for the world by Don Miguel Ruiz: (1) Be impeccable with your word. (2) Don't take anything personally.

(3) Don't make assumptions. (4) Always do your best. Please read Ruiz's book *The Four Agreements,* or visit his website, miguelruiz. com, for more in-depth study.

Group Activities CRADLING CEREMONY

When a baby or child never receives the warmth, nurturing, and unconditional love of a parent, she or he is left with a deep longing in the soul. The cradling ceremony is a way of providing that feeling of warmth and nurturing that was missing during childhood. This is a ceremony of the heart and can be created with variations depending upon the group. The steps are as follows: (1) Lay a king-sized quilt on the working floor space. (2) Assist the participant to lie down diagonally on the blanket, head and feet pointing to opposite corners. (3) Smudge/cleanse the participant and the surrounding area. (4) Wrap the participant in the same manner as bundling a new baby. (5) Gather helpers on each side and at the head and feet of the bundle. (6) Slowly pick up the bundled participant with arms locked underneath and across from each other. If possible, have two helpers at the head. (7) In unison, have the helpers gently sway back and forth like a cradle rocking in the breeze. You may play music or sing lullabies to the participant. (8) Have each helper whisper loving words of welcome in the participant's ear. (9) Gently set the bundle down on the floor and, with helpers still gathered around the participant, offer gifts in the form of blessings, prayers and songs.

WELCOMING HOME CEREMONY

Every soul retrieval is like a homecoming as parts of us reenter the body. Sometimes at WRC, we create spontaneous ceremonies to acknowledge and honor parts of the self that have been ignored, are in hiding, or feel like they don't matter. We create space for each person to share their experience with the group when they bring their soul part home. This ceremony can be especially powerful for veterans who have never been properly thanked for their service and welcomed home. As with all ceremonies, the welcoming home ceremony is created specific to the individual participant's life circumstances and needs for closure.

WAILING CEREMOMY

My elder teachers shared with me the importance of letting ourselves grieve and even wail. In most tribal societies, there were ceremonies and grieving songs that helped people move this energy. Sometimes at White Raven Center we feel called to create a wailing ceremony for this purpose, especially if the group is carrying heavy grief energy. To begin the wailing ceremony, someone needs to drum. In our group, this is usually Toby. As he drums, Floyd and I guide the participant to cover himself or herself with a blanket, hunch over, and begin walking clockwise in a large circle. As this person walks while guided by a volunteer, he/she begins to wail. Soon others join the walking/wailing circle, each supported by another participant. Everyone wails until all of the energy has moved and there is a shift of the energy in the room. Slowly, Floyd assists with each participant's transformation as they emerge from their blanket coverings and begin to dance. Again, this ceremony may have many variations. Spirit has a number of ways of creating opportunities for healing, and the wailing ceremony is one of them.

FAMILY SCULPTURING

Family sculpturing is a powerful tool that can be used to teach and recreate the dynamics happening within a participant's family system. It allows the participant to observe the roles he or she played, and continues to play, as a part of the family system in which he/she was raised. This role-play can give the participant insight into unhealthy cycles they have been recreating in their lives. Generally, it awakens emotions that have been hidden, which are now given an outlet for expression in the safe environment. This facilitates further healing. The observers and active supporting participants find themselves within the roles being enacted, within the characters being recreated. This often awakens emotions and brings to consciousness what is happening in their own families.

HO'OPONOPONO ~ HAWAIIAN CHANT

As with meditation, chants can be very powerful when done in a group. One that we love as a group activity at White Raven Center is the Hawaiian chant Ho'oponopono, which translates to "to make right, more right" or "to make righteous, more righteous." The chant includes the English words "I'm so sorry; I love you; please forgive me; I thank you." This version of the chant was shared with us by a friend, Leah, who had learned about its use from the spiritual director at the center where she received ministry training. She shared that it was used by a doctor working with mental health patients in a restricted setting. After chanting over his patients' files, the doctor noticed a miraculous shift in their healing—so much so that the hospital eventually closed, and the residents were either released or moved to a less- restrictive setting. To learn more about the origin and specifics of this chant, please visit the website www.sel-i-dentity-through- hooponopono.com or www.mindbridge-loa.com/hooponopono. html. This chant may also be done on your own.

DRUMMING, RATTLING, SINGING AND DANCING

The drum represents the heartbeat of all people. It can be a powerful tool that contributes to your healing. At WRC, we sometimes drum and sing songs to facilitate healing, either in the group or at individual sessions. Grandmother Falling Leaves says, "We rattle to shake away the old and drum to bring in the new." At White Raven Center, we ask each participant to share gifts of song and dance when they feel called to do so. If you are lucky, you may participate during a weekend when Floyd is teaching Alaska Native dancing and get to feel yourself transform into an eagle, killer whale, raven or wolf. I encourage you to listen to your own spirit's call for drumming, song and dance.

SURRENDER

Surrender is an important part of actualizing the full benefit of the RTT process. To capture the spirit of surrender at workshops, we frequently engage the group in singing the powerful surrender song that was gifted by Spirit to Toby Quinn.

When I don't know what to do,
I can't see the shore
When the wilderness consumes,
When the darkness falls

Surrender, surrender, surrender
Surrender, surrender, surrender...

To trust that I am the light
Surrender to my heart to restore my sight (x2)

When the mind has captured me,
Past and future's all I see
When the fear to lose control,
Controls... controls... controls...

Surrender, surrender, surrender
Surrender, surrender, surrender...

To trust that I am the light
Surrender to my heart to restore my sight (x2)
Restore my sight (x4)

To trust that I am the LIGHT!

FANTASTIC I AM

At the end of every weekend session, I lead the group in an exercise called Fantastic I Am. We all hold hands and swing them upward as we jump in the air, shouting three times: FANTASTIC I AM, FANTASTIC I AM, FANTASTIC I AM! This helps to shift the energy of the group and bring closure in a light-hearted way to a very intense weekend. This exercise and the words can be used on your own whenever you feel the need to lighten up. Fantastic I Am was taught to me in the Tlingit language by Kai Monture when he was twelve years old. The Tlingit words are *likodzi aya xhat*.

EVERY LITTLE CELL IN MY BODY IS HAPPY

After completing the Fantastic I Am exercise, Toby leads us in a cutesy little song to further lighten up the atmosphere and to help us celebrate the amazing work that has been accomplished over the weekend. The song that starts out at a slow pace is repeated over and over, increasing the pace until it is so rapid that it is impossible to sing any longer, and everyone is rolling with laughter. The words are: "Every little cell in my body is happy; every little cell in my body is well; every little cell in my body is happy; every little cell in my body is well. I'm so glad that every little cell in my body is happy and well; I'm so glad that every little cell in my body is happy and well" . . . and on and on. I invite you to sing and celebrate your happiness with this song. Make up your own melody.

Healing Our Selves to Contribute to Healing the World

WHITE RAVEN REMINDER

Practice paying attention and listening to the animals in nature. They are our friends and allies in restoring balance to ourselves and the planet. Like Raven, all animals are messengers of the universe. If we pay attention to them we will be the recipients of abundant gifts, in the same way we humans received the gift of light from our White Raven friend.

Appendix E

Recommended Reading List

You can read these books in any order; I have listed them in the order they were introduced to me.

Codependent No More by Melody Beattie
Co-Dependence—Misunderstood-Mistreated by Anne Wilson Schaef
When Society Becomes An Addict by Anne Wilson Schaef
You Can Heal Your Life by Louise C. Hays
The Way of the Shaman by Michael Harner
Soul Retrieval: Mending the Fragmented Self by Sandra Ingerman
The Seat of the Soul by Gary Zukav
Anatomy of the Spirit by Caroline Myss
The Seven Spiritual Laws of Success by Deepak Chopra
Yuuyaraq: The Way of the Human Being by Harold Napoleon
Excuse Me Your Life Is Waiting by Lynn Grabhorn
The Power of Now by Eckhart Tolle
The Four Agreements by Don Miguel Ruiz
The Mastery of Love by Don Miguel Ruiz
Mastery of Awareness: Living the Agreements by Doña Bernadette Vigil
Being Peace by Thich Nhat Hanh
A New Earth by Eckhart Tolle
Autobiography of a Yogi by Paramahansa Yogananda
Awaken in Time by Jacqueline Small *Waking the Tiger* by Peter A. Levine *Daring Greatly* by Brené Brown *Journey of Souls* by Michael Newton *One Spirit Medicine* by Alberto Villoldo

Appendix F

Acknowledgements

 Heartfelt gratitude to my mother, Julia Rolland, for modeling positive regard for all of our human sisters and brothers. Thank you as well for demonstrating love and care for the Earth and all her creatures.

 Thank you to my father, Siegfried Rolland, for sharing with me your gifts in the arts of communication, negotiation and inclusivity. Thank you also for passing to me your passion for the rich cultural heritage of Native American people and other indigenous peoples of the world.

 Thank you to my beloved teacher Grandmother Berniece Falling Leaves. You taught me far too many things to possibly include them all here, yet some are mentioned throughout this book. Above all, thank you for teaching and guiding me on the protocol for conducting sacred ceremony and for passing to me ancient rituals for healing. I feel you with me as I practice and pass on your teachings.

 Thank you to my teacher who guided me inward and introduced me to the profound methodology of core emotional healing, which has been the foundation of my work for the past eighteen years and the springboard for the evolution of RTT.

 Thank you, Grandmother Rita Blumenstein, for teaching me about the spirit world and trusting me with some of the ancient healing ceremonies and techniques of your people.

 Thank you, Martin High Bear, for sharing your medicine ways and offering to send me up the hill.

 To my beloved husband, Floyd Guthrie, a giant heartfelt THANK YOU for taking this incredible healing, writing, parenting and life journey with me. You continue to be by my side every step of the way and words are sorely inadequate to express the depth of my gratitude. To my children, Carly Ashby, Christina Ashby and Kayin Rolland, who I love as much as life itself. I am so proud of each of you for the individual healing work you have done for yourselves and the contributions each of you are making to humanity by following your life passions. Thank you also for giving up your private space one weekend a month for many years so that your parents could open their doors to the public and transform the entire family home into a healing center. How many children on the planet would make such a sacrifice?

Thank you to my gentle daughter-in-law Crystal Rolland for wrapping your graceful and loving arms around White Raven Center as you so beautifully help us maintain our sacred space to work with those in need of RTT services.

Enormous thanks and gratitude go to my amazing White Raven Center team: Toby, Rebecca and Rebecca, Zach, Stormy, Belinda, Claudette, Tish, and Cathy. You guys are a part of my dream come true. Each one of you offers so much in your own unique way with such grace, integrity and commitment. Thank you all from the bottom of my heart for your multiple contributions in the effort to provide a safe healing place for those who are suffering, which in turn led to the creation of this book.

Thank you to Ann Moller for your writing contributions and helping me gain clarity in my vision for this book. Thank you, Melanie Votaw, for the enormous undertaking of organizing the material for this book. My gratitude also for your willingness to conduct confidential and objective interviews of clients and for your writing contributions.

Thank you, Toby Quinn, for being so generous with your time and participation in the creative process, including sharing your surrender song with our readers. Your insight and writing contributions are invaluable.

Healing Our Selves to Contribute to Healing the World

Thank you, Rebecca Morino, for your loving support and astute help in proofreading the manuscript. Many thanks to Seth Taylor for your help with interviews and writing tasks. Thank you, David Taylor, for your encouragement, insight and support of this book project. Brothers, I deeply appreciate your active, passionate and tireless engagement with helping others find and pursue the RTT healing methodology.

Thank you to Kelly Notaras for guiding me every step of the way on this journey of creating a book; Kelly, you are an amazing talent and human being. Enormous thanks to Lisa Maloney for your editing skill and insightful scrutiny of this document to ensure alignment with truth, intent and clarity throughout. I honestly feel you are the only one on the planet that could have done this.

Thanks abundantly to Jack Armstrong for maintaining the White Raven Center website with pristine care and elite technical skill as this connects so many to the RTT work.

Thank you to John Tumelty for extracting from my soul a vision for the cover and interior design of this book, then jumping "down the rabbit hole" multiple times to make it happen.

Heartfelt thanks to Zachariah Fairbanks for sharing his poem, "The Forest Speaks", written while visiting the homestead land of his youth as he integrated his first experience of RTT processing. Finally and most importantly, abundant thanks to each and every client who has allowed me to share your story in these pages. There would be no book to offer if it were not for your willing courage to heal and to share your experience. And thank you,

Creator, for giving all of us the opportunity to experience life and healing on the planet at this time. Ah Ho!

✦